Poker
as Life

Poker as Life

101 LESSONS FROM THE WORLD'S GREATEST GAME

LEE ROBERT SCHREIBER

HEARST BOOKS
A division of Sterling Publishing Co., Inc.

New York / London
www.sterlingpublishing.com

AN *Esquire* BOOK

ESQUIRE POKER AS LIFE
101 LESSONS FROM THE WORLD'S GREATEST GAME

Copyright © 2004 Lee R. Schreiber

Cover Design by Celia Fuller
Interior Design by Elizabeth Van Italie
Illustrations by Jack Newman

Library of Congress has catalogued the hardcover edition as follows:
Schreiber, Lee Robert.
Esquire poker as life : 101 lessons from the world's greatest game / Lee Robert Schreiber.
p. cm.
Includes bibliographical references and index.
ISBN 1-58816-461-6 (alk. paper)
1. Poker—Psychological aspects. 2. Conduct of life. I. Title: Poker as life. II. Title.
GV1255.P78S37 2004
795.412'01'9—dc22
2004022464

10 9 8 7 6 5 4 3 2 1

First Paperback Edition 2008
Published by Hearst Books
A Division of Sterling Publishing Co., Inc.
387 Park Avenue South, New York, NY 10016

Esquire and Hearst Books are trademarks of Hearst Communications, Inc.

www.esquire.com

For information about custom editions, special sales,
premium and corporate purchases, please contact Sterling Special Sales Department
at 800-805-5489 or specialsales@sterlingpublishing.com.

Distributed in Canada by Sterling Publishing
c/o Canadian Manda Group, 165 Dufferin Street
Toronto, Ontario, Canada M6K 3H6

Distributed in Great Britain by Chrysalis Books Group PLC
The Chrysalis Building, Bramley Road, London W10 6SP, England

Distributed in Australia by Capricorn Link (Australia) Pty. Ltd.
P.O. Box 704, Windsor, NSW 2756 Australia

Manufactured in the United States of America

Sterling ISBN 13: 978-1-58816-685-2
ISBN 10: 1-58816-685-6

*This one's for
Alex & Amanda Hanowitz,
Andi & Zachary Schreiber,
and, especially,
my Ma—*

they're all Aces in my book

ACKNOWLEDGMENTS

*Special thanks to my editor, Matt Silver;
my publisher, Jacqueline Deval; my rabbi, David Granger;
and to my old school, the Wednesday Night Poker Game.*

Contents

♣   ♦   ♠   ♥

Foreword

By David Granger, Editor-in-Chief, *Esquire*

A s a species, we seem compelled to elevate our pastimes to the status of religion. We're forever trying to convince ourselves and other like-minded humans that whatever entertains us also teaches us life lessons.

For a brief time, back in the 1970s, tennis was like life. It was the game that best represented the essence of that era. The short-lived boom made it possible for such disparate (and minor) figures as musician-actor Dean Paul Martin (Dino's son and the tennis-playing lead of *Players*, the best tennis movie ever made) and Zenish author Tim Gallwey (*The Inner Game of Tennis*) to achieve some small level of fame and fortune.

In the 1980s, it was baseball that was like life. Big books by the likes of Thomas Boswell and George Will, and movies starring Robert Redford and Kevin Costner, made the impassioned case for the spiritual significance of our national pastime.

In the 1990s, of course, it was nothing but golf. You couldn't swing a 5-iron without smacking into some heavy literary/cinematic hitter peddling a key to the kingdom. It was either the collected wisdom of golf guru Harvey Penick in his *Little Red Book* or the mystic spirit of Shivas Irons in *Golf in the Kingdom* or the related movie version, *The Legend of Bagger Vance*, the worst golf movie ever made, featuring Matt Damon, Will Smith, and the exquisite Charlize Theron.

Now, of course, poker is the thing. The spread of its popularity likely began late in the last century with the appearance of *Rounders* (strangely, also a Matt Damon film), which inspired smart, cool young men to sneak off to clandestine house games or showy casino rooms to test wits and testosterone levels with each other. Players were also made at home, where they could watch demi-celebrities and poker gods playing televised pocket-cammed Texas Hold 'Em for huge stakes; or they could compete online against other computer-owning opponents around the world.

Poker is not just the latest fad; it has become our new national pastime. And because it is in human nature to believe that a real, true, lasting game is more than just fun or a lazy way to while away the hours between shifts at the plant or in the cubicle, this pursuit has taken on a life of its own, nourishing and depleting the spirit as well as the bankroll.

You hold in your hands a spiritual, yet earthy, guide to the betterment of intelligent life on this planet. Here, in one convenient bound, illustrated volume, is the accumulated wisdom of hundreds of years of cards, compressed and condensed by a writer who truly understands the game's mysteries and wonders. This book, like the man himself, is both playful and serious. The specific, hard-won, funny-profound "lessons" may be numbered 1 to 101, but their applications are virtually infinite. Here's palpable proof that poker is not only a lot like life, it is life.

Poker 101

Good, high-stakes poker players are neither noble nor greedy. They've sized up their fellow players, know a good deal about probabilities and tendencies, and wish like poets that their most audacious moves be perceived as part of a series of credible gestures.
—Stephen Dunn, poet, *Different Hours*

Poker has been a companion, a mistress, and a constant pleasure for most of my life. Nothing can match the adrenalized flush of a bluff in progress, or the cocksurety of a lock hand while your bettors expansively build up the pot. There is no greater game created by God or man.

I get all misty thinking about its many rituals: the glossy feel of a new deck, the crinkly sensation of scooping chips, and the pensive silences bracketed by the kibitzing din. I could go on about the scatological badinage, the arguments over Hoyle (and then, the camaraderie after the storm); not to mention the funny hats, cheap cigars, and staying up late.

Card-carrying proponents could make the case that poker has supplanted baseball as our nation's preeminent pastime; inarguably its interior game is one of the truest tests of character. Nowhere is the smell of burning synapses more acrid, or a person's mettle more easily forged and branded, than at the crucible known as a poker table.

Above all, poker is a great teacher. Its Pythagorean rhythms, Elizabethan drama, and Freudian slips surpass the depth and breadth of vitae found in virtually any other curriculum.

Like most profound subjects, it may appear deceptively simple at first glance. But the greedy, insatiable student will likely spend a lifetime of evenings trying to suss out its secrets. Ultimately, you will discover that poker is a mystery that eludes complete mastery.

During the course of your education, you will learn about finance (money management), mathematics (probability and odds), literature (playing by the book), human resources (getting along with—or even manipulating—disparate, often odious, personalities for the good of the game), and if you're a particularly quick study, you'll soon learn that poker is primarily about psychology, in which the perceptive, intuitive, and observant student of human nature will usually be materially rewarded at the end of a session (or a month of sessions), while the psychologically dense or unexamined will likely remain cash, and insight, poor.

These days, with televised tourneys far outrating major sports like hockey, even spectators can benefit from its tutelage. Every turn of a card reveals a deeper understanding of how the world works: in business (gamesmanship, salesmanship, negotiations, killer instinct, and power); in relationships (self-awareness, self-esteem, resilience, risk, and reward); and in, well, everything else (philosophy, fashion, nutrition, poetry, and politics).

In poker, as in life (and vice versa).

—L.R.S.

Poker
as Life

1. Talk the talk (before you can walk the walk)

This sucker's tighter than a nun's doodah.—Thomas Austin "Amarillo Slim" Preston, World Series of Poker champion, author, *Amarillo Slim in a World Full of Fat People*

Every line of work or play has a lingo all its own. If you want to keep up with the big boys, you must learn to speak their language. (Once you do, you can sit in with a company of players throughout the globe and pretty much catch their drift.)

Pokerese, the mother tongue of poker is downright Shakespearean, especially when you think of all the phrases that are rooted in its etymology: ace in the hole, beats me, blue chip, bluff, call your bluff, cash in, let the chips fall where they may, pass the buck, poker face, stack up, up the ante, when the chips are down, and wild card . . .

♠   ♠   ♠

This book is not a poker primer; we assume you already know the basics. If not, take some time to read a few good tomes like Lou

Krieger's *Poker for Dummies*, Mason Malmuth's *Fundamentals of Poker* and Mike Caro's *Fundamental Secrets of Winning Poker*. (Go ahead and do it now; we'll wait.) Herewith, to supplement your studies, is a short Pokerese—English lingo lesson, which we'll continue to run in installments throughout the book.

Pokerese

ace in the hole (*n. phrase*): 1. having an ace as a down card (usually in stud poker). 2. indicates a desirable condition, an advantage and/or a hidden resource kept in reserve until an opportunity presents itself.

ace out *(v. phrase)*: 1. to win, perhaps by bluffing, while (literally) holding an ace-high (or, figuratively speaking, a relatively worthless) hand. 2. in common use, can mean winning via deception or just barely beating out someone.

2. It's just business

Industry executives and analysts often mistakenly talk about strategy as if it were some kind of chess match... The real world is much more like a poker game, with multiple players trying to make the best of whatever hand fortune has dealt them.
—David Moschella, author, *Computerworld*

Poker can be fun, but it's not a nice, friendly game. It is brutal and primal, filled with duplicity and deception. It is not for the weak-kneed or the kind-hearted. You must play with rapacity and ruthlessness. You must play with a cutthroat cunning. You must play with one overriding rationale in mind: to accumulate someone else's—everyone else's—money.

♥   ♥   ♥

Despite all the good times you may share with your poker "pals," you have no allies during a game. No matter what the stakes—pennies, peanuts, or pot limit—everyone there is trying with every wile to deduct what is rightfully yours.

Be charming and gracious to all, but trust no one.

You can be, and should be, a kind, considerate, and trustworthy friend and neighbor in your personal life. But poker is not personal; it's business. And before you sit in, you must ask yourself: "Can I furtively shift from mouse to cat? Or gut an opponent without flinching?"

It is murder, prey tell, with a license to steal. By choosing to play, you're accepting those precepts.

You know the deal, now let's play some poker.

Pokerese

ace (card) up the sleeve (*n. phrase*): 1. in which a cheater surreptitiously withdraws an ace (or other beneficial card) from the deck, waiting for the right situation to take unfair advantage; 2. a generic description for any advantage (usually ill-gotten).

3. Take nothing personally

The air had wakened him and he saw clearly that this was no personal feud, this was a poker game.
—James Jones, author, *From Here to Eternity*

A guy steals your girlfriend: good riddance; obviously she wasn't the one for you. A competitor steals a client: no use being pissed at either of them; you've just got to work harder at customer relations. A poker "pal" steals a pot by lying (not with a well-constructed bluff, but an outright falsehood—see below): blame no one but yourself.

To unseasoned, unschooled players, taking complete responsibility for others' mistakes (and forsaking revenge on the miscreants) may sound wimpy or Pollyannaish; these greenhorns likely believe that poker is a macho, militaristic game that relies more on intimidation and payback than on patience and a turn-the-other-cheek philosophy.

They'd be dead wrong. (Well, half-wrong; intimidation is integral to the game.)

Poker rewards the exemplars of controlled aggression, not uncontrolled retaliation. If you allow any emotional considerations (especially anger) to drive your decision making, you will almost certainly lose. You cannot target any individual(s) for specific retribution. Let the poker gods do their job; yours is to leave any extraneous personal issues at the door; yours is to play your cards and your opponents in a calculatingly cold manner; yours is to maintain a rational, steady, energized, and consistent approach. And there you'll find your vindication.

♣   ♣   ♣

Case in point: Early in my poker career, as a college freshman, I was naïve enough to take a man at his word. When the Great Ike (a salute to his 300-pound size, not his poker acumen) repeatedly swore in the name of the King of Kings that he had me beat on board, that the two pair I had showing would not be good enough to win the pot, I folded. Then, with this huge smirk, he showed me his cards, which couldn't beat a dead mule. "I lied," Ike said. I had to be restrained from ripping out his cheating, lying, atrophying heart. Immediately afterward, I looked for any and all opportunities to burn his fat ass, which only led to loose, losing play on my part. In the end, it was my bad, not his. Only a damned fool would take a poker rival's blood oath at face value.

Now let's apply this thinking globally. It's rarely in your best interest to take anything that anyone does (anytime, anywhere) personally—not the competitor who undercuts your bottom price to steal away a client; not your boss who lowballs you at salary review time; not your (former) buddy who horns in on your girlfriend (okay, she was an ex-girlfriend at the time, but he should've asked for my blessing); and not the Great Ike, who was just using the best tool at his disposal to steal a pot.

Now, you may ask, what about hypersensitive human nature? What if you are constitutionally disposed toward taking offense at everything? What if you interpret even the most innocuous comment as a veiled insult, slight or criticism? Two bits of advice: 1) Get over it, 2) Don't play poker.

It's your call.

Pokerese

aces up (or eights up, tens up . . .) (*n. phrase*): highest of the two pair in a hand.

ace-to-five (*n. adj*): a version of lowball draw in which the Ace is the lowest card in the deck, straights and flushes are of no value, and the best hand a player can have is A-2-3-4-5 (which is also known as a *wheel*)

4. Don't get your knickers in a twist (or your panties in a bunch)

The cardinal sin in poker, worse than playing dead cards, worse even than figuring your odds incorrectly, is becoming emotionally involved. —Katy Lederer, author, *Poker Face*

The talk at the table, when it isn't poker related, consists mainly of insults masquerading as humor. Mothers, in particular, are fair game (even, sad but true, dead ones). This essentially harmless kibitzing can range from almost joyful noise—the basic parlance padded with colorfully indecent, incorrect, insensitive, and often incomprehensible banter endemic to your particular game—to the bitingly scabrous (and more universally recognizable) nasty needling that some players consciously deploy to throw others off their game.

As a result, fists may occasionally be raised, or chairs kicked away, in a heated moment. But cooler heads—usually attached to winning hands—must prevail. Everyone must realize that the good of the game is more important than some petty altercation. The game must be sustained, and any excessive tension, bickering, needling, or fighting will obviously not help (though it may be your intention, on occasion, to incite someone in particular to leave . . . and never come back.

♥ ♥ ♥

A good rule of thumb in all walks of your life: Lose the chip (on your shoulder). Manifesting anything more than passing anger in business, love, or life is self-defeating. It throws you off your game. It makes you fair game, because everyone (with the possible exception of tennis great John McEnroe) is less effective in an agitated state than in a clear, calm one.

Be aware: There will be agitators in every arena who, for their own self-driven purposes, will try to intentionally rile you (especially if they know that it doesn't take much).

Don't give them the satisfaction. Go to therapy. Go to anger management. Go to the beach for a long weekend.

In the end:

- The robust expression of short-lived anger is a luxury few of us can afford, be it in relationships, in business, or in any other areas of your lives.
- Your overly aggressive response could do more to precipitate, rather than prevent, future failures.
- Anger will ultimately hurt you more than anyone to whom you may express it.

5. Never complain, never explain

What's the difference between a puppy and a poker player? Eventually the puppy stops whining.—Anonymous

You will never receive, nor should you ever expect, any compassion or sympathy at a poker game. For one, nobody gives a flying crap; for another, any information disclosed can only, and will only, be used against you. That may sound harsh to the uninitiated; but you're there to play poker, not nursemaid. All feelings of sadness or loss there may be should involve only one thing: money. And even then: Shaddup! Who, but you, has any interest in that bad beat on the river?

Alas, it is equally true that (during a game) no other player is riveted to that detailed explanation of your crippling gout, your miserable sex life, or even your dying mother. (Save the drama for your mama, because in the poker world no one else cares.)

Keep all hardship to yourself. Take it like a man, even if you're a woman. And never, ever, not in this or any subsequent lifetime, share a single true feeling with your poker "mates."

♣   ♣   ♣

Sailor, one of the regulars in our Wednesday Night Game, once made the mistake of telling us that he thought the phenylalanine (Nutrasweet) in diet soda was making him impotent. That was four-teen years ago. Since then, not a week has gone by that some player has downed a beverage—any beverage—without some limp, scatolog-ical reference from the cheap seats. (And now, with erectile-dysfunc-tion-fighting medications like Viagra on the shelves, the cruel, unre-lenting wisecracks replicate open-mike night at the Comedy Store.)

The most honest, yet human, foible can be twisted—or spun—to your disadvantage (and someone else's advantage). The die-hard needlers, who interpret any vulnerability as a wound of weakness, will keep cutting just to watch you bleed.

Keep your conversational fodder (and mother) off the table. And, above all, keep your privates private.

Pokerese

act *(v)*: to make a play (bet, call, raise, or fold) in turn.

6. Shut up and deal

Some players are known as "specialists" at talking a good game—deceiving, intimidating and cajoling novices into making bad judgments and costly playing errors. —David Hayano, anthropologist, ethnographer, and author, *Poker Faces: The Life and Work of Professional Card Players*.

I n our weekly game, whenever anyone argues, cajoles, pontificates, or needles for too long, a guy named Lenny is on us like cheap cigar smoke.

"Enough with the table talk," Lenny says. "Shut up and deal."

♦ ♦ ♦

Amen, I say. ("Table talk" can be interpreted in one of two ways: as the usual jabbering and jabbing that accompanies most friendly games; or, more strictly speaking, as a pejorative term for arguably inappropriate verbal plays and ploys.)

This is probably a minority opinion, but I believe it's a terribly tacky tactic to try and *talk* someone out of a pot, as opposed to out-thinking or outmaneuvering him. Needling, however, is an accepted form of strategy in most weekly games (and, apparently, all televised tournaments, in which the noisome, bellicose chatter often seems like an audition tape for the WWE).

Even the savviest veterans can be thrown off (or "on tilt," in the current vernacular) by pinpoint needling. As a result, you'll see occasional evidence of testosterone-stirred tempers, rather than an evenly flush temperament, dictating actions. Instead of aiming for the ultimate prize—a pocket full of dead Presidents—their focus will be on a human target.

Certainly you want to keep a keen eye and ear on your primary competition; but, if it's not in the cards, you can't allow animus or any other extraneous motives to force a head-to-head matchup.

There is, in my opinion, only one legitimate reason for pulling out the needle: to drive an overly odious (or skillful) opponent from the game for good. The best way to do this is not to prod, poke, or pick at him incessantly and mercilessly (if he's winning he won't care), but to ratchet up the ragging after every *burn*. Be mindful, though: Your mark may not leave quietly, and possibly not before a punch or two is thrown in your direction.

The surest vaccination against needling is victory after victory.

7. You can observe a lot by watching

Everyone's got habits and you've got to recognize them. You know how cows always take the same path to the watering hole, one behind the other. Hell, even the beasts of the jungle, them elephants, take the exact same path when they go to die. Poker players are just the same. —Walter Clyde "Pug" "Puggy" Pierson, old-school card player, and World Series of Poker champion

Baseball legend Yogi Berra was a naturally friendly and guileless ballplayer. As soon as he'd reach first base, he'd start chatting with the opposing player about family, home, chewing tobacco, whatever . . . until he got the hit-and-run or steal sign. From that moment on, Berra would clam up and concentrate. Ralph Houk, his Yankee manager, wondered why Yogi was always being thrown out on pitchouts. (It didn't take long for opponents to pick up on Yogi's silence.) Finally, the Yankee skipper told Yogi to just keep talking at all times, no matter the situation.

♠   ♠   ♠

Smart players always keep their eyes (and ears) open to the opposition's tendencies—any verbal tics or mute manifestations of body language—that might emerge during the heat of battle.

What is he saying?

Even better, what is she thinking?

These priceless clues are called "tells," those telltale signs that unconsciously reveal the contents of someone's hand(s). Learn to look and listen beyond the bad acting and bullshit chatter to find the unadulterated truth.

As Yogi himself said: "You can observe a lot by watching."

Pokerese

advertise *(v)*: to make a point of showing cards after a bluff (indicating that you are capable of bluffing... or to relay some other piece of information), usually to set up players for a future misdirection play.

8. Tell yourself

Whether he likes it or not, a man's character is stripped at the poker table; if the other players read him better than he does, he has only himself to blame. Unless he is both able and prepared to see himself as others do, flaws and all, he will be a loser in cards, as in life.—Anthony Holden, author, *Big Deal*

I t's time to face facts. What do you see when you look in the mirror? A handsome, winsome fellow with dimples, much younger looking than his years? No? Let's rephrase the question: What is the predominant trait necessary for success in poker (and most other areas of life)? Psychological proficiency. Which means what exactly? A high degree of self-awareness.

How do you cultivate and elevate self-awareness? Study human nature. And what is the best way to study human nature? Find a human to study. Who? You. Who better? You come cheap. You have unlimited access to you. And you know you (or should) better than you know anyone else.

♥   ♥   ♥

To truly know yourself you must be capable of assessing your base traits in the harshest possible light (and then redress your failings). You must accurately gauge with complete objectivity your levels of perceptivity and receptivity; your reserves of self-esteem and ruthlessness; your response to adversity and good fortune; your need for approval, respect, and love. You can bullshit the rest of the world—that's part of every human's job description—but don't even think about bullshitting yourself.

At first your "you" may need some professional help. That's right, a competent psychiatrist, psychologist, social worker, therapist, counselor, or any other type of licensed mental-health practitioner to jumpstart the self-analysis. (Here's where women might have an advantage, their gender being historically more open to an organic expression of thoughts and emotions.)

Those males who've heretofore avoided exploration of our inner depths might need to heed this warning: Whereas in the personal arena you should allow your therapy-aided insights to more directly, openly, and kindly facilitate interaction with family, friends, and lovers; in more competitive venues, your self-knowledge should be primarily utilized in pretending to be someone you are not. You must spot your tendencies so you can learn how to suppress their free expression.

Let's say you prepare for a job interview by practicing how to stand, sit, speak, and shake hands in a prescribed way; but, as you lose yourself in conversation, conscious actions give way to instinctive behavior. Patterns emerge. You might clasp your hands together when you embellish a story; you might rub your chin when you become agitated; you might raise your voice when you're intimidated; you might smile when you pull a straight flush . . .

Stop. Assess. Redress.

It's like learning to play golf. All of those swing tips (grip, stance, takeaway, backswing, and follow-through) are confusing. Many of them seem unnatural. You may find that it's nearly impossible to play and think at the same time. Eventually though, with constant practice, your muscle memory takes over. You might need a reminder to trigger a certain move. But, essentially, you have taught yourself how to instinctively—subconsciously—take control of your thoughts and emotions. If you know yourself completely, you know what you're doing at all times. And then you can pay full attention to what your competitors are thinking, based on what they're doing (or not) and saying (or not).

Pokerese

Alexander *(n)*: king of clubs.

all black (or) **all blue** (or) **all purple** (*adj. phrase*): a spade or club flush.

9. Read between the lines

Know thyself—but don't tell anyone. —H.F. Henrichs, philosopher

Listen up. It's not just fish and pigeons that can be caught unselfaware with loose lips. Even Hall of Famers (like Yogi) may tip their hand with a few absentminded gestures and words (or the absence thereof). So if you can tune in to the sounds of the game, filtering out irrelevant white noise, the noxious needlers and trash talkers could be particularly vulnerable.

♣   ♣   ♣

As clever and provocative as their palaver may be, closer scrutiny will likely reveal some nuggets of valuable information. Chances are you'll need a substantial sample before you can arrive at a true hearing. But here are some oldies that are still pretty goodies:

What they say	What it means
Shilling for their cards.	If they point out their best potential hand ("four spades, possible flush"), they got *gotz*. (A kibitzer would likely get smacked for alluding to same.)
A "loud" call or raise either via voice or chips.	A lot of noise usually masks a weak hand; the intent is to intimidate with a big show.
Inappropriate jabbering.	This is a tricky one, but often the most telling. Some folks just like to talk; win or lose, their discourse is unceasing. Then there's the one (at least one in every game) who is unable to bluff and shut up simultaneously. He's yakking up a storm to drown out the nervous pounding in his head. (There's a classic M*A*S*H episode devoted to Winchester's major tell: Charles whistled when he bluffed.)
Silence.	On the other hand, when the constant chatterer goes mute, he's probably got the goods.

10. Information is power

The human element is the most important aspect of the game, and psychological deception often plays a key role in determining the outcome. In poker, opponents are seldom on the level with one another; it's typically to their advantage to be misleading. Perceptive players can steal the advantage for themselves if they know what to look for. By paying close attention to an opponent's mannerisms, both deliberate and subconscious, one can make an educated guess about the type of hand that person is most likely holding.—Mike Caro, author, *Caro's Book of Poker Tells*

I n the good old days, before poker crossed over into pop culture, the fish-pigeon-sap genus was oblivious to the concept of stealing signs (or of their captivity to be stolen). In my own little college corner, I had the "telling" field to myself.

♥   ♥   ♥

Here are a few tricks, and tics, I picked up way back when:

Angel was our (well, *my*) bluff-yak guy. I could listen to him all night. Most of the time, his conversational raps were typically soph-omoric—say, cogent reviews of the latest weed shipment. But, oh, every fifth or sixth hand, usually when the betting was light, he'd weigh in with a blast of bombast so loud, steady, and rambling that, for sure, he must have had some concealed I.V. hookah time-releasing squirts of THC into his bloodstream at prescribed intervals: "Scooch, whatcha got there, big guy? Looks like dreck bupkis to me, Hoss. You fill your boat with gas yet, Stinkaroo? Smells to me like your farts are a few ounces—heh,heh—shy. How'd you do on the geo midterm, Bunkbed [a nickname he made up on the spot for his roommate, Howie]? Betcha didn't ace it. Get it, guys? He's Louie [Jack], Bitch [Queen], Tendy [Ten] on board. Just needs the case bullet. [Well, actu-ally he needed a King, too, but none of us chose to correct his analy-sis.] Hey, how 'bout those Mets?"

At around "Hoss," my own potted synapses had picked up the code, and I tacked on "reraise" to Angel's table talk. I figured, Why let Bunkbed (Who? Ah, Howie) stick around to pull his miracle card . . . and make it very expensive for Stinkaroo—er, Lenny—to land his full house . . . ? Well, you get the point. Get rid of the competition (who probably had me beat) to go head to head with Angel.

After, say, my Nines-up took down his trifling two pair, he'd say: "Man, how'd you know I was bluffin'?"

"Lucky guess," I shrugged.

Little guessing, of course, involved there. Even less with Howie, a harmless blowhard who loved to brag about all the adoring, malleable "babes" he was stringing along. (Come to think of it, Bunkbed was an inspired nickname.) Whenever he had a good hand, he'd gently lay his cards on the table and start rubbing—more like stroking—his legs, from knee to thigh. I'm still not sure what this suggestive body lan-guage meant. Perhaps he was pantomiming the act of raking in chips.

Or maybe the only action he ever really got was in his hands (get it?). Whatever. All I knew was when Howie rubbed, unless I had a lock, I'd be gone. And that odd giveaway of his paid for all of my textbooks junior and senior year.

But Lenny (who later became a charter member of the Wednesday Night Game) was gold. Since nearly every dealer's choice was a high-low variation, a key component was the declaration, in which we announced our intentions by simultaneously opening a closed fist (1 chip or coin indicated a high hand, none for low, 2 chips or coins for pig, or both ways). If an observant individual chose to lock onto Lenny's fist a few seconds before he opened it, this person could predict with 100 percent accuracy whether Lenny was about to declare high, low, or both (fist facing down for high and both, fist facing up for low).

Think of the power and the riches in such a seemingly innocuous gesture. If one knew which way Lenny was going on every hand, one had so many more options at one's disposal: You could bully other players to fold and then, depending on the strength of one's own hand, decide to go against Lenny or accept half of the pot; as long as Lenny was in a hand (and Lenny was almost always in), it was like you had a partner in crime (except there was no partner and no crime).

For many, many years (from college until the moment he reads this account), that innocuous gesture has been worth thousands upon thousands of dollars to me alone. Now, out of a sense of duty and loyalty to my new readers, I free Lenny (and myself) from the annuity of his beautiful gesture.

Thank you, old friend.

11. Eliminate guesswork

Guessers are losers. —Amarillo Slim

Experts can often become dismissive when describing non-experts. Mr. Slim has been at the top of his chosen field for close to fifty years—he's played with poets, paupers, princes, presidents (LBJ and Nixon), and drug lords (Pablo Escobar)—so he's entitled to mouth off in overstated bites of bombast now and then. What the stellar self-promoter, and a damned fine player in his own day, meant to say (above) is that most successful people know their stuff so thoroughly, they're rarely in a position where they have to try to presume, hypothesize, or randomly surmise. Their educated "guesses"—informed by experience, instinct, practice, and skill—are usually right.

It stands to reason, then: In any mind-dominated game where an expert is pitted against an inexperienced, uninformed individual (a lesser guesser), the outcome is predictable.

♣   ♣   ♣

The following poker-specific predictors—gleaned from the work(s) of old pros like Slim, Mike Caro, Andy Bellin, and yours truly—are not always, absolutely, 100 percent correct, but when applied to a roomful of speculators they're pretty damned close.

Tells	Says
Throwing chips into the pot with an exaggerated motion, as if to say, "I'll see any bet you toss in there."	As with the "loud" call/raise the hand is likely a weak one; don't be fooled or intimidated.
Chip stacking.	Let me count the ways: When a player stacks the chips neatly and puts them into the pot, he's optimistic about winning them back; if he tosses them in willy-nilly, he's less certain of getting them back.
Betting hand.	A player might subtly give away his cards with the hand (the one with five fingers) he uses to bet: dominant hand when solid; other hand, when more speculative. Speaking of fingers, what does he do when he's not handling the cards? Is he drumming them nervously? Covering his mouth? Stroking his thighs? Pay close attention.
The quiet call/raise. Gently sliding chips into the pot, trying to slip them under the radar.	Good hand. Doesn't want to scare out the chasers.
Avoiding eye contact with opponents.	Trying to be nonthreatening—to downplay a strong hand, and to encourage a raise.

Tells	Says
Acting overly cool or blasé.	Anything that has "overly" attached to it is bad acting of one form or another; you must determine if it's a lousy, forced performance of an unhappy camper or a real portrayal of a bluffing fool.
Reaching for chips during an opponent's play.	Tricky one this: could be fake strength trying to scare; or genuine, unguarded enthusiasm chomping to bet/raise.
Covering your mouth during a bet.	Usually hides a poor hand, probably trying to avoid closer examination (psychological experts are divided over whether or not bad liars instinctively cover their mouths).
Staring intensely (or defiantly).	When a player looks directly at an opponent, he's usually trying to intimidate or threaten so you won't call his weak cards.

12. Shit happens

A man can find out a lot about himself, playing poker. Is he brave? Is he cool? Does he have any money left? —Martin Amis, author, *Experience: A Memoir*

Any moron can win a hand, but none can prevail consistently. One of the finest lines that separate long-term winners from steady losers is the capacity for resilience, the ability to bounce back after a crushing defeat, bad beat, or worse burn on a virtually locked—sure—hand that by all rights of probability and justice you cannot lose, but somehow, on the last turn or card, you do.

♣   ♣   ♣

What you do in the wake of disaster determines how well you do overall. How fast can you get your mind right? How soon do you move on?

You cannot control the vicissitudes of fate (what most people call "luck"), but you can control your response to them. Attitude is everything. How you deal with the daily beats and burns, the unexpected disappointments that belie odds and effort, will decide your destiny (or at least the perspective in which you view it). Wallow in the losses, become a victim of them, and they will assuredly mount up.

Shrug them off, suck it up, and you'll be ready when fortune turns in your direction.

13. Superstitions are stupid

I always wear black at major championship events, and you have to admit that my success is better than average. But does this make any sense at all? As a game theorist, I know that my chances to win are the same whether I wear black or white, but I have to admit to being a bit superstitious. —Phil Hellmuth, Jr., professional poker player and nine-time World Series of Poker champion

Who am I to quibble with the success of a Phil Hellmuth? If a black shirt and matching pants allow him to feel good about himself, thereby making him more likely to back up his cards with typical smart, intuitive, and aggressive play, then more power to him. Belief begets results. (But why wouldn't he wear the same outfit at all times, not just major events? Is he afraid of his juju fading with too many washings? Or is he just parceling his prayers, knowing they're more likely answered when you don't ask Him too often.)

A close reading of the world's great religions would find most prophets and holy men foursquare against false idols, trinkets, icons, talismans, and/or satanic ensembles. Yet, true believers of every stripe remain obsessed with finding the magical formula for instant karma.

Most of these so-called superstitious beliefs are universal. What plays in Peoria is likely *tocar en Pamplona*. Good luck, for example, characteristically befalls those who: knock on wood, walk in the rain, sleep facing south. And it's considered VERY good luck if: a ladybug lands on you. On the unlucky side (warning: those who swear by the black arts should probably avert your eyes), no good can come of: a bat flying into the house, violets blooming out of season, leaving new shoes on a table. It's EXTRA SPECIALLY bad luck to: kill a heron (particularly for the heron). On occasion, however, perspectives diverge, depending on your geographical POV. For example, in Spain, Belgium, and North America it is considered good luck for a white cat to cross your path (and bad luck when a black cat strays over); whereas, in Britain and Ireland, it's just the opposite: white cat, bad; black cat, good.

Do you sense some skepticism from this quarter? Damned straight. (If you want further cause for scoffing, turn to the dictionary: **su-per-sti-tion** n: *a belief or practice resulting from ignorance, fear of the unknown, trust in magic or chance, or a false conception of causation.*)

Some might say: "It's just harmless fun." And: "Couldn't a theological case be made for the wisdom of blind faith?"

I'd say to the last question: Only if it's a pagan faith rooted in medieval hooey. And to the first: It is *not* harmless. Every moment you invest on some pointless, godless ritual redirects or diffuses the effort you should be devoting to the formulation and execution of a smart, effective game plan (and to making adjustments as circumstances demand). Spending even a second on such nonsense can cost you considerable capital. There's plenty of harm in that.

♠   ♠   ♠

If you're still curious to know what (God knows why) a fool believes, here are an equal number of stupidstitions from each side of the aisle:

Good luck	Bad luck
Actors saying (or hearing) before a performance: "break a leg"... "knock 'em dead"... or "see ya on the green."	Actors saying (or hearing) before a performance: "Good luck."
Actors referring to "the Scottish play"... "that play"...	Actors saying (or hearing), "Macbeth." or "Mr. and Mrs. M."
A four-leaf clover.	A five-leaf clover.
An itch on the top of your head.	An itch inside your nose.
A naked woman on board a boat.	A dead woman on ship (I made this up).
A spider spinning in the morning.	Someone singing before breakfast.
Carrying an acorn, a rabbit's foot or a badger's tooth.	Leaving a house through a different door through which you came in.
Crossing your fingers.	Signing a lease or contract in April or July.
Dolphins swimming near a ship.	Stroking a calf on the back (bad for both of you).
Hearing crickets singing.	Hearing (or saying) the word "pig" while fishing.

Good luck	Bad luck
Killing a hedgehog (protection against bad luck).	Killing a ladybug, seagull, frog, robin, or badger (the latter is particularly bad for gamblers).
Meeting a goat on an important journey.	Changing a horse's name.
Picking up a piece of coal that has fallen in your path.	Picking up a coin, tail side showing.
Scissors hanging on a hook.	Cutting your nails on a Friday.
Seeing a white cockerel or a lone fox.	Seeing an owl in daylight.
Sleeping on unironed sheets.	Stepping on a crack in the sidewalk.
Sneezing three times before breakfast.	An owl hooting three times.
Spilling wine while proposing a toast.	Breaking a glass while proposing a toast.
Starting a round of golf with odd-numbered clubs.	Using golf balls with numbers higher than 4.

14. If you expect—or want —to lose, you will

Poker will also reveal to the frank observer something else of import—it will teach him about his own nature.—David Mamet, playwright/author/director

Losers may give lip service to the concept of winning, but they can't actually imagine themselves succeeding at anything. Worse, they put themselves into perfect position . . . to come in second, thisclose to victory, so they can curse their cruel misfortune ("What an unbelievable beat!") and wallow in familiar misery ("I can never catch a single break").

The only break these chronic losers needs is one in which they can take some time off to overhaul their entire emotional and philosophical outlooks. If they don't start to live, play, and work with true desire (and discipline), they will be condemned to repeat the same mistakes again and again.

♥   ♥   ♥

Take this hand of 7-Card Stud lifted from the archives of our Wednesday Night Game:

Lenny (3-hearts, 9-hearts in the hole) bets the high card (K-spades) on board—why, I can't possibly fathom (two semi-baby hearts?). Sailor calls with A-clubs and 7-clubs (down), 8-diamonds (up)—not much here either, but at least he has an ace and better flush and straight possibilities. Rosko, laying low with his pair of ladies (Q-spades showing, Q-diamonds and 2-hearts in the hole), just calls. Rich (10-clubs showing, his hole cards are irrelevant) raises; no surprise—Rich always raises. Three of us fold—none of us can beat the cowboy on board—while the three others call.

On Fourth Street Lenny is dealt 4-hearts; Sailor, 8-clubs; Rosko, 6-hearts; Rich, A-hearts. Sailor, now high with two eights (and that Ace kicker in the hole), bets; Rosko calls; Rich (a nickname—he's by far the richest guy at the game) raises. Everyone else—unbelievably—calls.

Fifth Street advances the action: Lenny gets 4-clubs (pair of sailboats on board); Sailor, 5-diamonds (no ostensible help); Rosko, 7-spades (ditto); Rich, 10-spades (high pair on board). Rich bets his tens; Lenny raises, trying (I'm guessing) to fake Kings-up, or three fours (Lenny's Lenny—there's no figuring his play). Rich raises again, and they all (even Lenny) call.

On Sixth Street, Lenny snags a four-flushing 5-hearts; Sailor, a 5-spades (two pair on board), and bets like he has the boat; Rosko, his second lady, Q-clubs, showing (and another one in the hole) calls; Rich, 6-clubs (his reign of terror over) folds. Lenny, with his four lousy hearts, calls.

The three remaining players receive their last cards down. Sailor, still trying to fake his baby boat, bets on the blind; Rosko raises the max. Lenny, the poor dear fool, reraises. We got a game.

Sailor has to look now—he figures Rosko for Queens-up and Lenny for Kings-up—and he thinks he's a winner after he squeezes out his A-diamonds, giving him Aces-up. Little does he know that Lenny, who had no business hanging around with his two 4's against two higher pair on Fifth Street (and then a possible boat with his four hearts on Sixth Street), has pulled his flush with J-hearts. Unfortunately for loopy Lenny, Rosko's last card (6-diamonds) filled his full house. After the laydown, their typical bleating begins. Sailor: "I can't catch one lousy, goddamned, fuckin' break . . . " Lenny: "Unfuckingbelievable. I pull the flush and still lose. Have you ever seen such miserable luck?"

Yo, guys, I hate to break it to you: It's your own misbegotten will, your dumb choices, your desire to bemoan and begroan your terrible, miserable, luckless fate . . . that put you into harm's way. You both should have folded after your first three cards, especially you, Lenny. At every point during that hand, you were a loser. And Sailor, you expected your two measly pair to hold up against a pair of ladies on board? Oh, sorry, you did pull that last bullet (just enough to come in third place).

I've gone a long way to prove a point. But it's a big one. Victims are unaware of how they've accepted victimization—it's so subtle and insidious. They blame unlucky circumstances or other, more fortunate, individuals for their lousy lot in life. They can't comprehend that they have the power to effect meaningful change. Why, guys? I'm betting: not enough self-esteem and too much fear. The bitch of it is: They could change, but that prospect scares them even more.

"What's the use?" they say. "It just ain't in the cards."

These prophets, alas, are predictably self-fulfilling.

15. Love yourself

The first thing a gambler has to do is make friends with himself.
—"Pug" Pierson

Huh? New-Age platitudes in a book about a metaphorical killing field? Uh-no. Under-the-table self-gratification? Ugh, no. This principle is about self, your essential self. Perhaps the prime requirement for winning at poker (or anything else) is a high level of self-esteem, the core certitude that you are worthy of success.

A lucky few are born with such inestimable, unshakeable belief in themselves. The rest of us who doubt our everlasting excellence and importance—or who occasionally feel deprived of sufficient love, affection, or praise—must battle harder to secure and maintain it.

Elevating self-esteem is an incremental process of small victories, of baby steps . . . and missteps. It's a constant struggle to fight fear, doubt, and your own deep-rooted demons. You must daily battle the alluring call to surrender.

During this process, you should try to surround yourself with positive people who provide nothing but encouragement and warmth. (Obviously that is not possible during the poker phase of this self-help program.)

Start by encouraging and praising yourself. Your "self talk" (verbalized or internalized) should always be upbeat. Fight all negative thinking. Instead of muttering bitterly about the lousy play that just backfired, think instead (please, please, never *say* any of these homilies aloud): "Nice try" or "Better luck next time."

Winning in increments will obviously go a long way to improving your self-image. But, ultimately, you have to care enough about yourself to do what is in your best self-interest.

Pokerese

aquarium (*n*): a likely place to find "fish" (poor players); usage in a sentence (or *phrase*): "Don't tap on the aquarium" (as in: Don't wake, or chase away, the "school" in session).

16. Two words: comfortable clothing

If you want us to give it our best, we'll have his underwear.
—Harry Vaughan, a White House aide, asking poker buddy (and boss), President Harry Truman, how to play it against purported pigeon, and prime minister of Great Britain, Winston Churchill

How good you feel—about yourself, your environment, your chances—plays a significant role in how well you perform. For the purposes of poker, and any other pursuit where your ultimate aim is "a satisfying or enjoyable experience" (the literal definition of comfort), your wardrobe can help facilitate that goal.

Fancy-schmancy. Lucky-schmucky. They don't have to be your best, most expensive or, as we've previously discussed (see No. 13), your most serendipitous duds. (Apparel, in and of itself, is made of natural or synthetic fibers; it is devoid of any serendipity.) You should outfit yourself only in loose-fitting, breathable attire that engenders ease of movement (even though your body will lack movement for long periods of time); in seasonally appropriate attire that sufficiently protects (and comforts); and in contingent layers that allow for all game situations. The latter instruction entails investigation of possible climatic conditions to be encountered en route, as well as a detailed familiarity with the interior of the destination environment, including any especially drafty or heat-absorbing pockets, in addition to the pertinent specs—construction material; fabric; pertinent height, width, and depth; extraneous markings; nail and/or screw protrusions—on the legs, back, and seat of every chair in the space.

For good hygiene (and neighborliness), wash and/or dry-clean every stitch of your ensemble from week to week, or game to game.

♦   ♦   ♦

There is one other piece of invaluable advice that you've heard before (though not here, and probably from your mother): wear unsoiled, antiseptic, tidy and totally intact undergarments. You never know when: (1) you might have an accident; (2) you could experience a health emergency; (3) the game will turn to strip poker; (4) the electricity might go out.

Blackouts do occur, and you might find yourself playing through the dark night till dawn (as we did during the Northeast's last great power outage,) with the only light on the block—a handy gas lantern—barely illuminating a roomful of seven sweaty, sticky, sulfurously smelly fellows in nothing but their skivvies.

The even unprettier sight of rank, raggedy, rudely sullied boxers (or, God help us, off-white briefs) could have made it our last game, instead of one of the all-time classics that we'll never forget (mostly in a good way).

17. Counter program

I think poker is all about acting. It's all about confusing the other players and tricking them into thinking you don't have a hand when you do, or that you do have a hand when you don't.
—Aisha Tyler, actress, *Friends*

I f actors are not among poker's best amateurs, they may be its most enthusiastic and prolific practitioners. Down time, a by-product of non-steady work, must be filled with pastimes; and, for years, poker seems to have been the show-business favorite. In addition, the nature of the game itself is a way of keeping the chops honed. What is bluffing and misdirecting tendencies if not acting?

I have played with many thespians, some really good ones, and I'm invariably amazed how many have been such bad actors at the poker table. (I'm also surprised when some hugely successful captain of industry can thrive in the boardroom, yet remain impossibly inept in the card room; I used to assume killer executives make killer poker players.)

I'm no actor (though in a college production of the Woody Allen short story, *Death Knocks*, I was referred to as a "second-rate Jerry Lewis"), but I do find the writing process in sync with the poker process. In fiction, you create believable characters with organic lives of their own; or, say, if you ghost-write a book purportedly authored by a famous figure, you must craft a "voice" from the transcripts (and ego) of your subject—often making him or her a hundred times more witty, perceptive, and wise on the page than in actuality—and then staying true to that character.

In poker, as in plays and movies (as in life), you have numerous chances to reinvent yourself; or, to play out various permutations.

♥ ♥ ♥

Years ago, I had to take a psychological test to land a corporate gig. I knew there was no shot if I answered honestly and directly (two qualities right there that would've disqualified me). So I imagined what, and who, the ideal candidate would be, and responded accordingly. I simply counter-programmed myself for a wider audience. I became Mr. Opposite. (Remember that episode of *Seinfeld* when George went against his basic instincts and uncharacteristically succeeded every time?)

I was no longer an introspective loner; I was a jovial team player. I valued obeisance over individuality. I preferred tranquillity to creative tension. It was the most fun I ever had on a written exam. And then I nailed the audition; or, as they called it, the personal interview. I got the job. (Fortunately the division merged after three months, and I was not offered another position.)

Unless you're a psychopath, it's impossible to sustain a false front for too long. Nor should you even try. But it can be invaluable to mix things up periodically, take on new and different roles. Always keep them guessing.

18. Get their attention— and keep it

I want all them players' eyes on me. I want them to sweat out what I'm doing. I want them all involved with me. And I'll do anything to get their attention. If you don't act the way you should, you ain't there. —"Pug" Pierson

Job #1 of every new guy: Get their attention. If nobody's watching, your subtle brilliance will be wasted. Somehow you must demonstrate to them (the ones who're accustomed to holding all the aces) that you're worth watching. You don't necessarily have to kick over the table to announce your presence. You don't even have to do much more than give them a small sampling of what you've got (or whatever you want them to think you've got). In poker, that's easily done by winning a few pots, and maybe once coming over the top with a reraise. Throwing in a few check-raises should also help get you noticed.

♠ ♠ ♠

Job #2: Keep their attention.

Here's a specific play-by-play blueprint that just might work:

Stack and restack the blue chips (or whichever ones are the highest denomination) whenever you run your first bluff. If it's a small pot, you won't mind getting caught. Or, if your bluff succeeds, openly show your cards (which is often done voluntarily, even in a cutthroat game). Later, you may "accidentally" flash them (you can't be too obvious—remember, these guys are good; they'll eat you alive if you make a mistake). It won't take more than two or three times for the sharks to smell blood. And when they do, you've hooked them.

You then choose the moment of truth—your most potentially profitable opportunity—by absentmindedly signaling your little chip-stacking routine. Throughout the hand, as you bet and/or raise, you never stop "telling," stacking and restacking. If all goes according to Hoyle, the sharks will slide out of the shadows after they let you build up the pot. (Note how the other fish are blithely sailing along, oblivious to any tells—pseudo or otherwise—and the imminent bloody confrontation in their midst; without ever getting the drift, they'll soon get out of the way when—likely, at the river's edge—the chum hits the fan.)

Wham! The sharks emerge with maximum teeth exposed, betting (or raising) the limit. "Dead meat," they're figuring. But you hit back: Wham-bam!! You come over the top at 'em, shooting with all barrels (the metaphors are coming fast and furious now, too) until you've successfully trapped and gutted every last one (or, at least, the greatest, whitest one) of them. If they're lucky, you let 'em slink off with a fin or two intact.

Rare and precious is the satisfaction. It's not just your victory; the entire free world celebrates when the underdog prevails, when David slays Goliath, when prey defeats predator. And priceless is your pleasure when you earn wads of cash and respect with such a singularly stunning and swift—and surprising—blow.

Pokerese

As Nas (*n*): An ancient Persian game often cited as one of the direct ancestors of poker.

automatic (*n*): play made regardless of one's cards, often in a situation where the bet wins; **automatic** (*v*): literally, as in a blind, an automatic bet.

baby (*n*): a small card, usually a 2,3,4 or 5 (add an ace or a 6, and you've got a **baby straight**).

back (*vt*): to provide funds for another player.

19. Surprise!

Those of us who have not been trained to deceive have a tendency to cover our mouths or avoid eye contact when telling lies. That's why I've never dated an actress. —Andy Bellin, author, *Poker Nation*

It takes a vast, regenerating repertoire of masterful, Machiavellian moves to amaze, astonish, and astound. It takes perceptiveness, intuitiveness, and imagination. It also takes great patience to lay (or lie) in wait and then strike folks dumb, catching them off guard and/or making their heads swim. That's *all* good stuff.

♦   ♦   ♦

But: the ingenious, self-gratifying ploys that pay off in the shark-infested worlds of poker and business don't usually play as well in your personal life (where any chameleonic, manipulative persona is often non grata).

And: if you have the capabilities to surprise smart, suspicious people, you're less likely to be startled or shocked yourself (again, good in business and poker, not so good in private).

Plus: If you're accustomed to controlling the action, you're probably not comfortable letting your guard down, or allowing yourself to be vulnerable to anything unplanned.

Romantic relationships, in particular, necessitate a capacity to surprise someone else, as well as enjoying it (and her) when she surprises you. Somehow unanticipated thrills are sweeter and more thrilling than those you see coming. And who doesn't want a mate with the requisite smarts and brass to provide the ineffable joy that only comes from a bolt out of the blue?

It's a delicate dance to find that perfect balance in your professional and personal lives—to be able to take others by and yet still be open to the exquisite possibility of unexpected pleasures.

20. Boys will be boys, but it's not just a man's game

To return to the question of why some men will not play poker with women. Is it because we are less scientific and, by not paying attention to the odds, thereby upset their calculations?
—Barbara Tuchman, historian and Pulitzer Prize-winning author, *The March of Folly: From Troy to Vietnam*

B
efore we address Ms Tuchman's question—though my immediate answer would be, "Nah, I don't think so"—here's an old poker story. (Warning: some profanity and blasphemy.)

In a $500-$1,000 Hold 'Em game at a large casino, one player had consumed too much alcohol.

"That was one piss-poor card you turned, you dickwad!" the drunk said to the dealer after missing his club flush.

"Sir," the dealer said, "there is a young lady at the table. Please control your language."

On the next hand, the drunk's two pair lost to a straight on the River. "Jesus Christ! Goddamnit!" he cried.

The dealer had reached his limit: "Sir, I'm telling you for the last time; there is a young lady at the table. Control your language, or you will be physically removed from the table."

The next hand, every player waded into the pot for the flop. Then there were numerous raises and reraises until the drunk lucked into an inside straight and about $35,000. He asked the dealer, "Do you guys pool your tips together or keep them for yourselves?"

"We keep our own gratuities," the dealer said.

The drunk tossed two $500 chips at the dealer and said, "Well, then, enjoy this little gratuity, you asshole!"

The dealer picks up the $1,000 and turns to the young woman at the table, "Miss, please take your uptight snatch out of this casino."

♥   ♥   ♥

Maybe it's social conditioning. Maybe it's the Machiavellian component or the testosterone-saturated compound found in the Y chromosome. Maybe it's even a fallacy. But poker has usually been perceived as a male bastion, both as sanctuary and arena.

The thinking goes (or went): At the end of a hard day, men like to kick back, loosen their ties, or put on their schoolyard best—T shirts, sneakers, jeans—and play. And it's gravy if they get to kick some figurative ass in the process.

Wherever men have gathered, they've vied to be King of the Hill. Or Ace of the Whole. And, in this pursuit of domination, they've schemed, plotted, cursed, sulked, whooped, farted, belched, and even bonded. Boys have been—and, presumably, will always be—boys.

Rightly or wrongly, women have been perceived as a threat to the male's inalienable freedom from responsibility, the commitment to immature behavior, and the need for space. Poker has been a respite and refuge . . . from jobs, relationships, the ruins of battered dreams. As such, historically it has been—and, in some smoke-filled hovels, may still be—a man's game. (Some hard-boiled character once said to another: "A deck of cards is like a woman—usually when you pick one up, you wish you hadn't.")

Some men (not me) don't even like women to visit a poker game. Bad juju. We used to play in this big-time agent's office atop the Carnegie Deli in midtown Manhattan. Beautiful actresses (and models taking meetings to upgrade) would drop by constantly. Every week we'd be introduced to a Meg Ryan, a Saundra Santiago, a Kirsten Dunst, or whoever the hot young thing at the time was. "Yeah, whatever," we said, barely looking up. "Deal the cards." There was one stunning starlet who even wanted to sit in. You should've seen those accomplished men stammer and phumpher the lamest excuses, not because they were necessarily nervous around a pretty woman, but because they wanted to prevent her from visiting our males-only club and possibly report back to her sisters.

My feeling is: If they've got the cojones—and the cash—to take us on in our house, we should be able to keep our secrets safe for a night. Even with all of the inherent bluff, bluster, and brutality, an immutable fact of poker life remains: The right-brain skills such as flexibility, imagination, and, especially, intuition—those so-called feminine traits—pay off with far greater frequency.

21. It takes all kinds

The great pyramid of gamblin': sharks at the top, then the rounders, the minnows, and at the bottom the fish—the suckers, the suppliers. Scavengers and suppliers, just like in life.
—"Pug" Pierson

There are several basic poker archetypes, variations of which can be found at almost every regular/weekly game extant (all bets are off when describing the top professionals), including: 1) the Fish Called Lenny, who's really just a nice guy born to finish last; 2) Mr. Testosterone, who sees poker as a test of manhood, refusing at all costs to be bluffed out, and/or who bets on every card in every hand as some misplaced act of aggression; 3) the Chaser (or Sailor), who is strictly there for the action, and doesn't care if he wins or loses; 4) the Burn Victim, who lives to come in second—to be badly burnt—so he can bemoan his cruel fate without taking any responsibility for his own lack of acumen and discipline; 5) the Needler, who tries to throw you off with his incessant japes and barbs; 6) Slim (or Doc), who is the man to beat.

♥   ♥   ♥

Which one are you?

If you ain't Doc, or Slim, or somewhere close to either, you need to lose your old nickname, and the piss-poor game that came with it.

By the way, there's a good rule of thumb that can identify the sucker at the table even before the first hand is dealt. Is there a fellow called Lenny sitting there?

In all my years of playing cards, it seems that, oh, maybe 75 percent of the time, there's been a Leonard, Len, Leonardo, Leo (but only when it's short for Leonardo), Nardo, or Lenny in on the action. And assuredly, it is action he wants. He will bet on every hand like it's nobody business; he will rarely fold, and, unsurprisingly, he will lose almost every time out. Why Lenny? It's one of the great poker mysteries in life; I can't explain it. Years ago, when I went through a rough patch, I was so down on myself that I started to think maybe "Lee" belonged in that ignominious company. But I soon picked up the scent again, and never gave it another thought. Besides Lee is my full given handle; there must be a Leonard/Leonardo root for the name-blame-game to work.

The kicker is, each Lenny, Len et al. I've known has been a decent, sweet, genuinely good guy (which, of course, usually means loser at poker). If "Slim" or "Doc" sit at the head of the poker pantheon (see page 70), then "Lenny" resides at the opposite—or rear—end. (If, by small chance, there is no person actually named Lenny in your game, it is deemed proper—albeit gratuitously cruel—to dub the nicest, sweetest, chasingest player by that classic poker moniker.)

Tough luck, Lenny. I don't make the rules. I just report on them.

22. Emphasize empathy

I believe it is probably true that women on the whole are not inclined to discipline their playing according to a scientific law of averages. Speaking only for myself, I find that the incomparable advantage of playing by instinct is that no one else has the slightest idea what I am likely to do or why. —Barbara Tuchman

Let's take the feminization of poker even further—beyond science, beyond probability—into the realm of instinct. In order to make educated guesses about an individual of whom you have little or no prior knowledge, you have to rely on your ability to understand, be aware of, be sensitive to, and vicariously experience the feelings, thoughts, and experience of another individual without having the feelings, thoughts, and experiences fully communicated to you in an objectively explicit manner by that individual.

In lay terms: You have to identify with your subject.

In even layer terms: You have to get inside someone else's head (even if it's nothing like your own) and imagine what makes him or her tick.

♣   ♣   ♣

Historically (anthropologically?) women have had a leg up in this area; presumably their instinctual wiring enables them to plug into other people's feelings, thoughts, and experiences with far greater accuracy than, say, men. This intuitive disposition can be leveraged to great advantage in numerous quarters, poker being one.

If you are not, by nature, an empathetic individual, you must be willing to work on this deficiency either on your own or with the help of a proven professional. You must summon more than trash talking and macho posturing when digging deep into your duffel of tricks. (If not, find a new bag.) Somehow, and soon, you must discover a way to interpersonally connect with others (or come up with a foolproof method on how to convincingly fake it).

In short: When the chips are down, you must learn to think and feel like a woman.

23. If you laugh, it's funny

Tragedy is when I cut my finger. Comedy is when you walk into an open sewer and die. —Mel Brooks, actor/writer/composer/director/comic genius

You have to actually be there to appreciate the genuinely amusing playfulness and occasional brilliant wit that's elicited at the poker table (though, in retrospect, most players would be hard-pressed to recall the most inspired, sidesplitting moments). Jokes and comic routines are fine, but the best, funniest material is invariably found on the spot, off the cuff. This cutting humor depends on context, and how fast you can twist or exaggerate reality and rattle or poke loose your neighbor's pomposity. Maybe it's the testosterone; maybe it's the cutthroat competition. But cruelty seems to be the comic form in which most lines are delivered (though, as Mel indicates above, one's man haplessness is another man's hilarity).

♠   ♠   ♠

The free flow of language is too colorful, raw, and darkly humorous for the mass taste of broadcast television. It's not just the cursing that would turn the FCC on full tilt; it's the scatological, sophomoric, anti-authoritarian strain of comedy that screws everyone left and right, royally. No subject is out of bounds; no one is spared. Everyone and everything is fair game: racism; the Holocaust; slavery; AIDS; even dead mothers (especially dead mothers). Bad taste is irrelevant. Political correctness is for pussies.

All's fair . . . as long as it's funny.

Pokerese

beat on board (*phrase*): when the up cards held by other players (or by community) are better than the ones you have in your hand; it's probably a good time to fold.

bee deck (*n*): a deck made by the American Playing card company, and called such because of the large bumble bee found on the ace of spades.

Beer hand (*n. phrase*): a Texas Hold'Em hand where the first two cards dealt to a player are 7-2.

24. The fundamental things apply

Never play cards with a man named Doc. Never eat at a place called Mom's. Never sleep with a woman whose troubles are worse than your own. —Nelson Algren, author, *The Man With the Golden Arm*

Sweeping generalizations are rarely beneficial in a world constantly in flux. However, Algren's popular, oft-paraphrased axiom, coined circa 1950, has thoroughly penetrated high and low culture; his comment is as likely to be found in a fortune cookie as in most academic anthologies of famous quotations. Its relevancy has never lagged, probably 'cause it addresses three of the 21st Century's most viable topics: poker; food, and sex (and not necessarily in that order).

Like many brilliant sayings, Algren's actual words have shifted slightly over time. Sometimes you'll see "Never play cards with a man named Doc" (who is, on rare occasions, replaced by "Slim") switching places with "Never eat at a place called Mom's" (or, sometimes, "Ma's"). Regardless of position, the first two dictums are probably more viable now than they've ever been. Who can even find a place called Mom's? Virtually all Mom (and Pop) neighborhood operations are being inexorably run out of town by landlords looking for bigger rents, franchises looking for a little toehold. and malls looking for national anchors. (The homogenization of America will not be stopped.) As for the physicians, they're being squeezed dry by the huge insurance and pharmaceutical giants; it's becoming harder and harder to find an actual Doc who can afford to sit in at a substantial game. And where are the new "Docs"? No, not the board-certified M.D., the D.D.S., or even the Ph.D ... but the up-and-coming *Doc* (the nickname reserved for the preeminent player) in the poker community. Occasionally you come upon an old Ace or even a venerable Slim, but when's the last time you sat in with an operator worthy of the nickname—a "surgeon" with steady hands, supreme tactics, and instincts that can gut *and* empathize.

♣   ♣   ♣

Me, myself, I've never played with a bone fide Doc. The last one I heard of was the fearsome, deadly John Henry ("Doc") Holliday, a dentist by training but a poker player and marksman by instinct and trade. Doc died in 1887, at age 36, so he never crossed paths with Nelson Algren, but his best friend, Wyatt Earp, hyped his sidekick's myth with this rave review: "He was the most skillful gambler, and the nerviest, fastest, deadliest man with a six-gun I ever saw." (In his final moments, Doc asked for a glass of whisky. Which he then drank, said, "this is funny," and died, maybe the last true Doc of 'em all.)

Holliday had a checkered history with the ladies, so he's no help when trying to expand on the embodiment of Algren's final rule of three: "Never sleep with a woman whose troubles are worse than your own." The writer himself, inaugural winner of the National Book Award for *The Man With the Golden Arm* (Frank Sinatra played the drug-addicted-stud-poker-dealing, protagonist in the movie), was perhaps the first guy to famously reject his own brilliant advice. In fact, Nelgren's troubles with women were legendary. In 1937 he married Amanda Kontowicz; subsequently he divorced, remarried her, and divorced her again. In 1947 he embarked on a 17-year-long trans-Atlantic love affair with the French writer and feminist Simone de Beauvoir, who never left her life companion, existentialist author Jean-Paul Sartre (even though he was reportedly a lousy lay); Algren felt betrayed and hurt after she published details of their stormy relationship. In 1965 he married Betty Ann Jones; they divorced two years later.

Whether Algren heeded his own words or not is irrelevant. Embrace the aphorism, not the aphorist. And while he stopped at three "Nevers," here are a few more that should serve you well:

Never eat Chinese food in Oklahoma.

Never insult seven men if you're only carrying a six shooter.

Never murder a man when he's busy committing suicide.

Never play cat-and-mouse games if you're a mouse.

25. Never say never

A player who never bluffs at poker is not in sympathy with the game. —William J. Florence, author, *The Gentlemen's Handbook on Poker* (1890)

That (No. 24) is all good advice. Make that great advice. However, because contingencies are essential to any successful plan, absolutes should probably be avoided.

♥ ♥ ♥

Examples:

"Never play cards with a man named Doc." Never? What if Arthel Watson—the flatpicking guitar and banjo legend, blind since the age of one—walked through the swinging doors to your parlor, and asked to sit in at your poker game? Would you turn him away because you had no deck of Braille cards? Not if he was game to go, you wouldn't. And would you run scared because, as a fan of his music, you knew that people have been calling him "Doc" since he was 19? Probably not. If you're a liberal-minded man or woman, you'd play with that 80-year-old sightless warbler and you'd take his money.

"Never eat at a place called Mom's." You'd eat there—and you'd eat plenty—if that mother was the late, great gourmand Julia Child.

"Never sleep with a woman whose troubles are worse than your own." Let's just throw out a few names of the most stunning beauties of all time: Helen of Troy. Cleopatra. Vivien Leigh. Marilyn Monroe. Jacqueline Bisset. Julia Roberts. Natalie Portman. We can't say for sure how troubled these ladies were/are, but we can speculate that their problems, on balance, might have been/be greater than yours. If you'd kick any or all out of bed, you're a much better man than I (and no doubt more deeply disturbed than anyone could've imagined).

Pokerese

big blind (*n*): The larger of two forced bets in Hold 'Em, for the player in second position. The amount is equal to the top betting increment at the table (for example if you are playing $1-3, the big blind would be $3).

26. If you can't figure out who's the worst player at the game, it's you

Think about what it's like sitting at a poker table with people whose only goal is to cut your throat, take your money, and leave you out back talking to yourself about what went wrong inside. If you don't believe me, then you're the lamb that's going off to the slaughter. —Stu Ungar, professional poker player and World Series of Poker champion

If Principle No. 24 isn't the most renowned poker-related adage ever opined and transcribed, then it is this one: *If you can't figure out who's the worst player at the game, it's you.* Its author, though, remains unknown and uncredited (which is entirely fitting since the greatest old-school players typically preferred the anonymity of hidden wealth and inner satisfaction to fleeting fame and IRS notoriety).

The basic theme has seen dozens of permutations, among them:

"If you're in a card game and you don't know who the sucker is, you're it."

"If you're playing in a poker game and you look around the table and can't tell who the sucker is, it's you."

"In the first ten minutes at a poker table, you want to assess the competition—the best and the worst. If, at the end of that time, you still can't figure out who's the lousiest player in the game, get up, go to the bathroom and look in the mirror. The worst player at the table will be staring back at you."

It's often very difficult to admit that you suck at something, especially when all along you thought you were such a hotshot. But: All is not lost. The first step is acknowledgment; then, acceptance; and, finally, activation of the plan that will turn your game, and your life, around.

It can be done.

Oddly the individual most frequently cited with popularizing this principle is Paul Newman. The Oscar-winning actor and motor-racing champion is himself not known for having a particularly avid or winning poker game, but he has starred in at least three first-rate movies (*The Sting*, *Nobody's Fool* and *Cool Hand Luke*) that contain plot-driving poker plays. In the latter flick, Newman's Christ-like character, Luke, got his nickname after bluffing out a fellow inmate with nothing.

"Sometimes," Cool Hand Luke says, "nothin' can be a real cool hand."

27. Hold the phone

If we shoot him, we won't have anyone to play with.
—Jimmy Stewart, actor, as Wyatt Earp in *Cheyenne Autumn* (to Doc Holliday about what to do with a card cheat)

If someone is involved in life-or-death work, there's a good reason for him or her to be accessible at all times. A potential emergency is another legit rationale. But what about the people who've got cell phones stuck to their ears day and night? (Or headphones? What the hell are they listening to during a poker game? Yanni? Doyle Brunson books on tape? He's sitting right over there, dipstick. You want to know something, ask him.) Why this compulsion to be connected to some disembodied voice? What's your problem?

MOST LIKELY, THEY ARE:
- insecure conformists, who must keep up with the pack;
- afraid of being alone (or of being alone with their thoughts);

- deluded about the importance of their work;
- whipped;
- degenerate gamblers.

WHAT THEY ARE NOT (WITH THE POSSIBLE EXCEPTION OF WHIPPED):
- first-rate poker players.

A first-rate poker player is a true individualist—a lone wolf —who listens to his own voice above all others. He is not much impressed with the resources required to afford a mobile phone, or with the know-how needed to operate it, or with the teeming and professional social circle obligated to monopolize it.

♦   ♦   ♦

There is no call that anyone must make or take at a poker game, not to or from: your mother; your bookie; your guru; your model-actress girlfriend; not even if it's from the authorities informing you that your dear ol' Ma has died (she'll still be dead when the game ends).

So, please: no interruptions, no interference, no excuses, and, above all, no irritating sampling of lame songs whenever the damned thing rings. Play cards, not DJ or social director.

28. The stakes must hurt

If nothing is at stake, what's the point? —Gus Hansen, professional poker player and World Series of Poker champion

There's no point in playing if it doesn't mean anything. Meaning can be found in any number of ways: money; property; a physical test, an emotional challenge, or a simple enjoyment of the process.

♠   ♠   ♠

In poker, it's all about pain: the pain of a meaningful loss (i. e., losing your shorts, your balls, your prestige, your savings, your house). Your objective is to protect your hand. You protect a good one by making them pay to see it; you protect a bad one by making it hurt even more to see it.

The idea of playing for fun (i. e., no possibility of meaningful loss) is oxymoronic. How can you bluff someone out if there's no risk in the outcome? It's not Russian roulette if you don't use real bullets. And it ain't poker if you don't use actual money (or a representative equivalent).

29. No balls, no blue chips

Money is just the yardstick by which you measure success. In Monopoly, you try to win all the cash by the end of the game. It's the same with poker; you treat chips like play money and don't think about it until it's all over. —Chip Reese, professional poker player

B ack in the day, blue chips were always the highest denomination (simply white, red, and blue—in ascending order). The "new" traditional order at most major casinos seems to be: $1, white; $5, red; $25, green; and $100, black. At the next, and highest, denominational level is the $500 chip, which is most often tinted—get this—purple or lavender.

No cojones, no purpureo?

Whatever the color of your money, the philosophy is the same: The more you risk, the more you can make (and, of course, the more you can lose). You certainly can, as a stone rock in a low-limit game, grind

out a nice, tight-fisted income. But if you ever decide to step it up a hue in stakes, and in competition, you've got to upgrade your mental game as well. That means: more bluffing and semibluffing, more check-raising, more calling and, at the core, more and steadier nerve.

Pokerese

big slick (*n*): in Hold 'Em, A-K as one's hole cards (a.k.a. **Santa Barbara**).

blind (*n*): in Hold 'Em, a prescribed bet put in by a player before he gets his cards. A blind is part of that player's bet if he comes into the pot, as opposed to an ante, which immediately "belongs" to the pot." A blind can be mandatory or optional.

bottoms (*n*): cards dealt illegally from the bottom of the deck.

30. Don't throw good money after bad

It is well always to remember the words of the philosopher: "It isn't whether you win or lose, but how you play the game." I would like to meet that philosopher. I would like to invite him to our game. I would like to hold, say, three queens against his three jacks. And I would like to make him a bet that he would quit being a philosopher. —Russell Crouse, playwright, *State Of The Union*

Y ou can't control the precise amount you win in a poker session; the cards, the streaks, the trends, the breaks, and your overall level of play will collectively arrive at a specific number. You can, however, control the exact amount you lose. Well before you arrive at the game, you determine a figure. It can be based on numerous factors, but the most important ones should be: How flush you are? How much can you afford to lose?

♥   ♥   ♥

Once you've established the loss limit, it's final. You reach it, you walk. Period. End of discussion. No amount of cajoling, kibitzing, whining, or "guilting" by others (and no rationales offered by any inner voice) will convince you otherwise. There's no point wondering what might, could, or should happen if you stick around. It's very possible that your terrible luck will reverse (or that Lenny's will), but you absolutely should not be there to find out. And no, you don't want to stay and watch—a player wants to play.

Minimizing losses is a constant in any solid, disciplined game plan. In business, you don't waste valuable time or money trying to fix equipment or manpower that is irrevocably broken (and you don't look back unless it's to learn from your mistakes). Similarly, in relationships, you're advised to invest your time and effort, not your ego. If you're doing all the work, move on.

In any and all events, cut your losses as soon as reason, not emotion, dictates.

Pokerese

bracelet (*n*): the coveted piece of jewelry awarded (along with the prize money) to the winners of every event in the annual World Series of Poker held at Binion's in Las Vegas.

31. God is in the details

I don't think anyone has done the right movie on poker yet. It's something that really has to be touched by a great poker player, and I don't know whether it will ever get done. —Vince Van Patten, actor/director, *The Sopranos*

It's always the little things—in life, in poker, and in art. And if the minutiae don't ring true, then the whole thing begins to fall apart. Nowhere is that truer than in movies, where a single false note—be it in the acting, directing, screenwriting, photography, editing, scoring, production design, costumes, continuity, and gaffering—among other elements—can sink an entire production. If a film enters any realm of specialized expertise—say, baseball, psychiatry, and unidentified flying objects—the toughest critics are the so-called experts.

In poker, every player is a critic.

We asked a few actor-players for their favorite poker-related flicks.

"*Rounders* was a nice attempt, but it still didn't do the right job exactly," Vince Van Patten says. "I got to give credit to Steve McQueen—the attitude he had as *The Cincinnati Kid*, and the whole New Orleans feel of that film, was quite excellent. Even though it wasn't a great movie, there were great aspects of it. So, I'm gonna go with *The Cincinnati Kid*."

Lou Diamond Phillips also chooses *The Cincinnati Kid*. But his favorite poker line, "Sometimes nothing is a real cool hand," is from *Cool Hand Luke*.

Emily Proctor likes a line from *Maverick*, his seventh rule of poker: "Never play with a woman."

Here is the definitive, as of now, Top Ten, worst to first:

10. *The Cincinnati Kid* (1965). Overrated. The finale is so bogus it ruins winning performances from McQueen and Edward G. Robinson.

9. *The Music of Chance* (1993). *Cincinnati Kid* meets *The Prisoner*. Offbeat psychological tale—grim and funny—adapted from Paul Auster's "existential" novel. Extra credit for presence of M. Emmet Walsh.

8. *Kaleidoscope* (1966). A little-seen diamond in the rough starring Warren Beatty as a playboy-card shark who marks the world's playing cards in a way only he can read (don't ask). In the showdown finale, against the narcotics kingpin, the doctored cards are replaced. And everything rides on Beatty's own wits. Who wins?

7. *Run* (1990). Law student Patrick Dempsey takes it on the lam after accidentally killing a crime boss's sleazy son. In one of the climactic scenes, a thug forces Dempsey to draw one card instead of standing pat. Talk about bullying a game.

6. *The Sting* (1973). Not really a poker movie, but the setup to one of the tastiest, twistiest plots in movie scamdom occurs during a game on a train when fake-boozy, "needling" Paul Newman out-cheats dour, dastardly Robert Shaw, thereby setting the sting in motion.

5. *House of Games* (1987). Mamet debuts as director of his own knowing, stylized, overly talky screenplay about a psychiatrist (his then wife, Lindsay Crouse) who gets taken to the cleaners and beyond by a group of con men, many of them real-life poker buddies who would become regulars in Mamet's movie troupe.

4. *Dr. Mabuse — Der Spieler* (The Gambler) (1922). Part I of Fritz Lang's silent masterwork. Loopy master criminal determined to use mind control on opponents to, say, fold a winning hand. Best line is the question asked upon entering a private club: "Cards or cocaine?"

3. *Rounders* (1998). Predictable plot and cardboard characters can't ruin the most realistic poker action ever filmed. John Malkovich excels in another scenery-demolishing not-*so*-bad-guy turn.

2. *A Big Hand for the Little Lady* (1966). This one is stolen by Newman's real-life wife, Joanne Woodward. Big fun. Big caveat, though: During a (the) hand, she's allowed to leave the saloon and walk out into the street with her cards. Not in a million years, lady.

1. *California Split* (1974). A favorite of degenerate gamblers, because it essentially shows a few days in their lives. George Segal and Elliot Gould play dead-end Gardena poker players happily born to lose. (Look for Amarillo Slim in a featured role.)

32. Find the poetry

A man who can play delightedly on a guitar and keep a knife in his boot would make an excellent poker player. —William J. Florence

I

t's good to know that, even in a world where immutable precepts and cold calculations reign, you can always find a measure of poetry.

Poetry in poker?

Abso-freaking-lutely.

There's poetry in Pokerese—evocative, even lyrical, descriptions found at every turn (and river); bad burns begetting worse beats; befuddling bluffs beggaring belligerent bumps; baby boats ballasted by bullets (and don't get me going with bupkis up the yin-yang).

There's poetry in the play itself: a foundation of metrical rules, laws, and ethics on which is built a free range of visceral creativity and innovation.

Above all, there's poetry in the epical struggle to avoid or cope with inevitable loss.

Ah, loss. It is the great theme of all Romantics who continue to rage against the dying of the light even, when a cataclysmic end is certain. You can forestall it with a brave struggle and, on balance, more victories than defeats.

◆　◆　◆

Poker's highest rewards are reserved for its poet-warriors who can battle with great ferocity; and yet, when the battle is over—win or lose—can retain their humor, perspective, and compassion.

Pokerese

buck or **button** (*n*): the marker used to indicate the deal position. (Once upon a time, an actual buck knife was used.) The common phrase, **passing the buck,** derives from this usage, though it more often means to shift responsibility to someone else.

bullet (*n*): the most popular slang term for an ace.

33. Find your groove

Poker is as indigenous to America as jazz, and full of just as much improvisation. —David Carr, writer, *The New York Times*

Think of it as the music of chance and skill, a blend of rhythms and styles—classical, standards, rock, and jazz (with the occasional blues mixed in).

Once again, there is a set of universal notes—a canon to which all must adhere. But within that framework there's all kinds of room for each player to move and/or groove.

♠   ♠   ♠

What kind of player are you?

Improvisatory—who likes to veer off the charts, taking cues and riffing off the men and women at each session.

Traditionalist—who studies the works and beats of past masters, and sticks close to their lines.

Eclectic—who is comfortable in any environment, high or low, and prefers not to limit his range.

Amateur—who is undisciplined, unschooled, and lacking in ambition, preferring to remain in a limited comfort zone without really testing his/her potential.

Atonal—who flaunts the rules and thrives in chaos, squawking and honking in constant disharmony.

All players (even rank amateurs) can alter and stretch their chops, providing they put in the necessary practice time and remain forever open to risk, change, and growth.

Pokerese

bump (*v, n*): used more in home games than in casino rooms to indicate a raise.

burn (*v*): 1. to take the top card out of play by dealer, usually by placing it face down among the discards (in Hold Em, a card is usually burned before each round is dealt). 2. (*n*) the card that is burned, or discareded, by the dealer in Texas Hold 'Em.

34. Explore T.H.E. greater possibilities

Hold 'Em is to stud what chess is to checkers. —Johnny Moss, legendary old-school poker player

Texas Hold 'Em (T.H.E.) is a fine variation—nasty, brutish, and easily condensed between commercial breaks. But it is not, by a long shot, the only game in town; nor is it necessarily the best showcase of a player's skills. (Because T.H.E. stakes should be high—optimally, no limit—both Joe Pro and the Average Joe can lose their bankrolls to some yutz with the nuts who's always wanted to say, "All in.") No less an authority than the great Pug Pierson prefers limit five- or seven-card stud, because he believes "the best player always wins and there is less room for disaster."

My personal favorite is some variation of seven-card stud high-low; it rewards the disciplined tactician who knows that it's a sucker's play to stay with the highest cards (with which you can only go high);

whereas, with low cards, you can win low, as well as with the occasional aces-up. But the real money is to be made filling into baby straights and flushes, where you can go both or pig. Win one or two of these big hands (more people tend to stay in and build up the pot) and you're on your way to a big, big night.

Before T.H.E. became the rage, a youngster coming up had a broad, liberal arts-range of virtually limitless dealers' choices. True students of diversity were served. Then T.H.E. tourneys on TV came along, and impressionable rookies began to play the same pro's game again and again.

Variety and unpredictability can spice up every aspect of life. Try new things. Kids, please, before it's too late: There's time to broaden your knowledge, disrupt your rut, and disband—and expand—your comfort level. There are dozens of (relatively) conventional stud/draw, high/low variations (with numerous twists and turns, buys and replacement cards, passed and common cards) that can supply equivalent bang for your bucks. If after a few rounds the games you know begin to leave you listless, create your own. That's how it's done all over the world. Someone gets a flash of inspiration and says, "Hey, let's try a new one, guys."

♦   ♦   ♦

Our Wednesday Night Game invented WOOLWORTH'S (well before the company's recent liquidation). It's essentially seven-card stud with some add-ons: Each player is dealt four down cards. You can immediately discard one card; keep two down and turn one (for free). Or, if you choose to keep all four—two down and then flop the next two, in betting order—it costs $10 (or an amount commensurate with your overall stakes). To keep only two cards (both down)—discard two and immediately get another one face up in betting order—it costs $5. It sounds a lot more complicated than it is. Oh, and the name:

Five-and-ten, Woolworth's. Get it? We also improvised a cheaper five-card ($4, $8) version called K-MART.

Note: The crazier and more convoluted the game, the bigger advantage for the good player. While everyone else is still trying to figure out basic strategy—which you intuit immediately—you're already controlling the game with advanced play.

Only one hard-and-fast rule: no wild cards. Ever.

Pokerese

buy-in (*n*): 1. minimum dollar amount required to get into a game. 2. amount of money (or chips) with which one starts a session.

buy the pot (*v. phrase*): to match the amount of money in any given pot.

"by me" (*v. phrase*): another way for a player to check or pass on a particular bet.

35. No limit is for losers looking to get even (and for winners, it's often no win)

If you [the best player] get off kilt, you're in jeopardy, you jeopardize too much money, the sucker can pluck you off.
—"Pug" Pierson

In our regular Wednesday Night Game, the last hand of the night is always the same: No Peak/No Bet. Everyone (usually seven players) throws in $20, and we're were all dealt seven down cards. Then, in betting order, without looking, we each turn 'em over one at a time, stopping with the high card(s) before moving on to the next player until his hand is best or he taps out. It takes about four minutes to play one game, and winner takes all ($140).

It became so popular that some guys (the losers) wanted to play an entire round of NP/NB.

They liked the idea of even-money (well, actually 7-1) odds to get back some of the cash they'd lost over the past several hours to better players. Even fools such as them knew that they had a better shot at a no-brainer than in any game in which skill, daring, and discipline were de rigueur.

Steady winners such as myself play one, maybe two, hands of NP/NB before calling it a night, while invariably three or four hard cases are left, steadily raising the stakes.

Now I'm not comparing a no-skill crapshoot like $20 No Peak to No-Limit Texas Hold 'Em (the pros' predominant preference). But there is an infinitesimal similarity that disturbs a pros' pro like Pug Pierson: too much at stake for too little skill.

"When you're a limit poker player and you're the best player," says Pug, "at the end of a time period, the end of a day, the end of a week, you're gonna wind up with your end. Luck is always gonna break even. . . . But if you're playing table stakes, when all the money in front of you on the table can be bet, then one little mistake can cost you your whole bankroll."

No-Limit Texas Hold 'Em will likely remain *the* game when it comes to final-table poker preeminence. It plays well on TV. The pros love the action. And every get-rich-quick-thinking amateur thinks he can buy in and win it all. (Occasionally, he does.)

Remember, any sucker can pluck you for one hand—whether it's for $20 or $2 million. Why give him the opportunity?

36. There's no such thing as luck

In the long run there's no luck in poker, but the short run is longer than most people know. —Rick Bennet, author, *King of a Small World*

The notion of luck, per se, is for losers. It's the easiest thing to blame when things go poorly.

"You dropped a bundle, Hoss. What happened?"

"Bad luck."

The mathematical and philosophical facts indicate otherwise: There is no such thing as luck (bad or good). Shit happens (see No. 12). That's life. Deal with it. By the end of your mortal run, unless you've been specifically targeted by some higher power (see the Bible: Book of Job), your stuff should break about even, give or take.

♥   ♥   ♥

Streaks, on the other hand, definitely do exist. They run good and bad, hot and cold, "lucky" and "unlucky" (for lack of better terminology). Your job is simple: maximize the hot streaks; minimize the cold ones. How you do that is up to your discipline, your nerve, and your Maker. It is the choices you—and only you—make that will ultimately determine your fate.

You make your own luck.

Pokerese

case card (*n*): the one remaining card (say, the fourth ace) that has not been exposed to a single player or to all players.

chase (*v*): to play loosely and buck the odds (possible origination: to chase rainbows).

check (*v*): to eschew a bet; if everyone checks, you get the next card(s) for free.

37. Imagine

There is such a thing as absolute premonition of cards, a rock bottom surety of what will happen next. A good poker player knows that there is a time to push your luck and a time to retire gracefully, that all roads have a turning. —David Mamet

---

Athletes refer to the feeling as being "in the zone." Some describe it as sort of a Zen mindset. True believers claim the power of prayer. It has also been called positive thinking, visualization, and mind over matter.

♦　♦　♦

We've all experienced this phenomenon at least once in our lives: the unshakeable certainty that something good is about to happen ... and then it happens. It could be the phone ringing (you're convinced it's the cute girl accepting your invitation to the prom). It could be your boss calling you into his office (you're positive he's offering twice the cost-of-living increase your coworkers are getting). It could be a split-second before the overtime field goal is kicked (you're so sure your team is going to the Super Bowl—while just covering the spread—that you barely even raise a cheer).

See it, and be it. Believe it, and achieve it.

Before you can be successful in any endeavor, you must be able to imagine it in your mind's eye: closing the deal with the cute girl; closing the deal with your boss; closing the deal with the one perfect card. If you can envision positive things occurring, then you can also conjure up an image of your victory celebration.

In poker, there are lengthy periods (sometimes entire nights) replete with those special moments when every hand fills in; when every move you make goes right; when your intuition and feel for the game are uncanny and unerring; when you simply cannot (and will not) lose. There's no credible, logical explanation for your streak, but there are few sensations as memorable or magical.

Think of it as an arbitrary gift from the gods (never believe you're ever due, or owed, anything from any One) that enables you to perform at the highest level with a minimum of conscious thought. Think of it as a clear, clean state of detached engagement (or engaged detachment). You are so thoroughly prepared, and yet completely relaxed. You experience the certainty and joy of your own (and/or a higher) power. How do you precipitate this mindset? You don't. You can't. If you try too hard for something, if you wish for or want anything so much, you will probably only ensure failure.

Get out of your own way.

Let it be.

Just do it.

Play the cards as best you can, and let the chips fall where they may.

38. Hoyle knew squat

When in doubt, win the trick. —Edmund Hoyle, author and originator of the *Hoyle* instructional book series

According to popular myth, Edmond Hoyle, Esq., was *the* poker authority, and his imprimatur, "according to Hoyle," retained its authoritative meaning well after he died.

♥   ♥   ♥

Whereas in actual fact, Hoyle was all hype.

Contrary to conventional wisdom (which is a good place to be in most pursuits), the London-born author did not codify the rules of poker—he died sixty years before the game likely originated. Nor was he, in all probability, a lawyer (though that supposition might have helped nail down the book deal).

Hoyle was a renowned, adept whist player, and his original book, *A Short Treatise on the Game of Whist* (1742), remained the gold standard for over 120 years until the Arlington and Portland clubs adopted new rules in 1864. Hoyle also wrote a succession of treatises on piquet (a two-handed card game played with 32 cards), quadrille, and backgammon (the first English codification), and his name and reputation ultimately became synonymous with the "highest authority" on virtually all card- and board-game rules. Many modern encyclopedias of poker still use the proverbial Hoyle name in their titles, though most of 'em aren't worth squat.

Pokerese

check-raise (*n* or *v*): a play in which a player initially checks; then, after someone else makes a bet, raises. It is usually considered a tactical, aggressive act designed to maximize the money in the pot, or to scare opponents out of the pot. In some "friendly" games, check-raising is verboten.

chop (*v* or *n*): 1. to split the blinds; 2. also synonymous with **rake**, amount taken out of each pot by the house.

39. Play by the book

The English Hoyle (*Bohn's Handbook of Games*) made no reference to poker in either its 1850 or its 1887 edition.
—Frank R. Wallace, author, *Poker: A Guaranteed Income for Life by Using the Advanced Concepts of Poker*

Which book?

As we've just seen, Hoyle didn't write it; he couldn't even read *Cotton's Complete Gamester's* (published in 1674, when Hoyle was 2) that included a description of post and pair, a forerunner of bragg, which preceded poker. Around the time Hoyle was developing his whist rules, several French academics were writing precepts for their homegrown game, poque, a direct antecedent of our beloved pastime.

Frank R. Wallace, author of the seminal (if Machiavellian) *Poker: A Guaranteed Income for Life by Using the Advanced Concepts of Poker*, cites 1850 as the likely date for poker's print debut—in *Hoyle's Games* (published by H. F. Anners, Philadelphia)—with "a brief note about poker that described a full deck, ten players (therefore, no draw), and a bonus paid for any hand of trips or better." The first mention of draw poker, Wallace says, was the 1867 edition of *Hoyle's* (Dick and Fitzgerald, New York). "Also, that edition was the first book to mention an ante, a straight (which beat two pair, but not trips), and the straight flush (which beat four of a kind)." According to Wallace, the first recorded rules were written by General Robert C. Schenck, the United States Minister to England, where "Schenck poker" was popularized due, in large part, to Queen Victoria's interest.

♦　　♦　　♦

Of course the phrase "playing by the book" is not meant literally literally. It usually describes consistently superlative play—sound instincts backed by a solid but aggressive approach with a healthy dose of unpredictability. But, from Hoyle to Wallace, it is the written form (on paper or screen) that a player seeks for codification of play. And the overall oeuvre has never been more prolific, or as proficient. We're now living in the Golden Age of Poker publishing, and here are some contemporary titles of the first rank:

- *The Greatest Game in Town* by A. Alvarez;
- *Super System* by Doyle ("Texas Dolly") Brunson;
- *The Body Language of Poker* by Mike Caro;
- *Big Deal: A Year as a Professional Poker Player* by Anthony Holden;
- *Hold 'Em Excellence* by Lou Krieger;
- *Positively Fifth Street* by James McManus;
- *Moneymaker: How an Amateur Poker Player Turned $40 into $2.5 Million at the World Series of Poker* by Chris Moneymaker with Daniel Paisner;
- *Zen and the Art of Poker* by Larry Phillips;
- *The Theory of Poker* by David Sklansky ;
- *Thursday Night Poker* by Peter O. Steiner.

40. Know when to go against the book

Gets down to what it's all about, doesn't it? Making the wrong move at the right time. —Edward G. Robinson, actor, as Lancey Howard in *The Cincinnati Kid*

Say you're a relatively tight player, a reluctant bluffer, on a serious roll. Everything is running your way. Your moves are impeccable; your cards are sure. You're in the catbird seat, and you're going to enjoy the ride for as long as it lasts.

How do you play it? (Hint: This is not the time to ease up on the accelerator.)

You don't throw the book out entirely, but you definitely edit it. Your so-called table image is sky high, which means your opponents are wary, if not scared, of you. Your bets now have greater power. This is the ideal opportunity for a semibluff, if not an all-out, throw-caution-to-the-four-winds bluff or (if it works) two. (To switch transportation metaphors: When your ship comes in, and your fellow deckhands are scrambling for a lifeboat, take full advantage and drown the poor rats.)

Say you're a loosely aggressive player, a frequent bluffer, in a serious slump. Everything is running against you. Your moves are peccable; your cards are cold. You're (back) in the passenger seat, careering out of control.

How do you play it?

When your table image teeters, you don't push it. Your opponents can all smell blood, and you're the chum, chum. What's the likelihood you can pull off a dead bluff? .001 percent (and that's only because two guys named Lenny are at the table). So, there's really only one way to play it: tight. You grab the wheel and hold on. Which means: You find out where the brake is located (and maybe even start using it). Which literally means: You play fewer hands. And if things don't break your way, you book. Which means: You consider your long-term portfolio and think about leaving early. That is to say: Get up. Go. LEAVE!

♦   ♦   ♦

There really isn't one 1000-percent, always-right way to play in all situations. Circumstances must be accommodated. Attention must be paid. You learn your way by nature, by experience, and by feel until you reach the outer limits of your potential. And by then, maybe you'll write your own book.

41. Go with your gut

Have you ever felt you had ESP (extrasensory perception) when calling a player's hand? —Phil Hellmuth, Jr.

Some experts call poker a counterintuitive game, citing as proof the vast majority of brilliant minds who cannot grasp even the most basic concepts, while pointing to the unschooled, grammatically challenged country boys who here consistently topped the tournament heap for years.

Yo, eggheads: It don't take a genius to figure out that shit ain't shinola and book-smart ain't necessarily card-smart. And: If you lack intuition, you can't win at poker.

♠   ♠   ♠

You either have it or you don't (a talent for drawing, writing, calculus, and cards). You can improve your game, whatever it may be, but you can't make a top-shelf bird from chickenshit.

For those of you with the gift: nurture it, develop it, hone it, and heed it. Listen to your instincts; they're usually right.

For those of you who're not sure if you have it, see what happens when you analyze less and intuit (ascertain stuff relying on direct knowledge or cognition without evident rational thought and inference) more. Sniff around a subject, rather than take it head-on. (Again, women may have an advantage here, experienced as they are in accessing unfiltered, unintellectualized feelings and emotions.)

For those of you who don't have it, and never will, you might want to think about a different pastime—like bowling, tiddlywinks, or whist.

Pokerese

community cards (*n*): face-up cards shared by all players.

dead man's hand (*n*): aces and eights, all black (the cards that James Butler "Wild Bill" Hickock was holding when he was shot in the back of the head by Jack McCall on August 2, 1876, in a Deadwood, Dakota Territory, saloon).

42. Lose your gut

If one lacks the discipline to throw away poor starting hands, then all the knowledge in the world can't overcome this flaw.
—Richard D. Harroch and Lou Krieger, authors, *Poker for Dummies*

Nothing against the corporeally challenged—I could stand to drop a couple of pounds myself—but the good, obese poker player is an anomaly. The discipline and motivation required to keep one's weight down are the same qualities that tend to reduce financial losses.

There are times when you're going to be tempted, particularly during periods of struggle and adversity. Your desire to cave—to break ranks and surrender, or to revert to old, failed tactics—may be overwhelming. It's natural to seek familiarity and comfort. It's easy. But while easy may temporarily satisfy your cravings, it won't feed the bulldog. (Huh?)

Let's put it another way. Short-term solutions never resolve fundamental problems. And another. To grow (emotionally) you often need to battle your first instinct. In other words, the courage it takes to impose unflagging discipline is not always instinctual; more frequently it arrives only after fear, fatigue, and/or fat have been confronted and conquered.

True bravery is tested every day in many mundane ways: eschewing that slab of chocolate before bedtime; refusing to be sucked into a marginal hand; fighting on when all seems lost (or gained).

♥ ♥ ♥

Quick Tips for Game Day: Avoid foods rich in tryptophan, a sleep-inducing amino acid found in proteins such as turkey and milk. Try not to snack on sugary or caffeinated goods during any important activity or event; the quick rush will inevitably lead to an enervating crash. (If you must partake, don't stop; to maintain the buzz, you'll have to keep shoving that crap into your face.)

Pokerese

dead money (*n*): cash or chips put into the pot by players who've folded.

43. No slouching, no slouch; no slumping, no slump

Each game you sit down you learn something, about yourself and about the opponents. —David Spanier, author, *Total Poker*

Start right off (and start off right) by sitting up straight. And stay there . . . for a couple of key reasons.

Good posture shows good discipline. They each feed off the other. And? Your physical demeanor—observed in individual parts or collectively—is a huge tell. In unguarded moments, especially when you're physically or emotionally tired, your body language can mirror the strength or weakness of your hand. The backbone (obviously) is often the first to go. You'll likely sit upright, or even lean forward, when you're eager to enter the fray. You'll likely hunker down, with round shoulders lowered, when you're half-heartedly engaged. (Of course, like some high rollers, you can pay a massage therapist to knead your aching back, keeping it straight, solid, and relaxed without much effort on your part.)

♠ ♠ ♠

If you start out by sitting up straight—and stay there—you'll appear like a winner (even when you're not).

Pokerese

declaration (*n*): the announcement, either verbal or, more often, demonstrated by the number of chips held in each players' hand and shown simultaneously, indicating which way (high, low or both) a player is going.

drawing dead (*v. phrase*): when a player remains in a hand even though it cannot possibly be improved.

44. Live the lie

A lot of players want to bluff in their mind, but in their heart they just can't push the chips out there. You have to convince yourself of what you're doing. If you don't really believe it, it shows.
—Johnny Chan, professional poker player and World Series of Poker champion

Bluff (v): *to deter or frighten by pretense or a mere show of strength; to feign; to deceive (an opponent) in cards by a bold bet on an inferior hand.*

Bluffing is what separates the strong from the weak, adults from children, and poker from virtually any other "game." You can win with the worst cards. Herein justice and injustice go hand in hand.

Every time you bluff, you're attempting with a well-crafted con to steal a pot that rightfully belongs to someone else. The twist here is that you can do it full view of your marks.

Pulling off the perfect crime, however, is hard work.

It takes a faultless setup, pinpoint timing, and the nerves of a burglar. It takes extraordinary patience to lie in wait for the opportune moment. Specifically, it takes the right number (few) and type (tight) of opponents; a characteristically tight (or on a night when everything is running your way, high) table image; relatively high stakes (in order to bluff successfully, you have to bet so it hurts); a small to medium-sized kitty (too much money at stake, and even the tightest players might be tempted to call); brilliant, underplayed acting ability; and the capacity to convince (or delude) yourself that you should, must, and will win.

That last point is worth repeating: You must believe. You must portray a consistent, fathomable, and/or reasonable portrayal of someone who(m):

- has the best hand;
- is about to scoop up all the chips;
- it would be foolish and unprofitable to call.

♥   ♥   ♥

Bluffing is not for the squeamish, the fearful, the transparent. You want to win all of your bluffs, but smart money says you cannot expect to collect on more than half. Hence, you will lose the other half. You don't have to like it, but you do have to accept it. There's no harm in getting caught in a lie (bluff); and there's no harm in (occasionally) folding a winning hand. Shit happens (a lot). Unless, perhaps, your name is Herbert Yardley.

Yardley was a World War II espionage operative and a poker maven throughout his life. He wrote about the confluence of his professional and personal interests—and a sliver of difference between the two—in *The Education of a Poker Player* (1957). In it, he claims to have pulled off the same bluff 41 consecutive times before he was called. In five-card draw, he bet or raised on the openers, took no cards, then wagered the maximum.

You're thinking: Brilliant move, sure, but how deaf, dumb, and dim would his competition have to be to fall for the same routine—not once, not twice, not even on 14, 23, or even 33 separate occasions—41 straight occasions. Admittedly it wasn't always against the same players, and it took place over a number of years, but C'mon.

Anyone for 42?

Pokerese

face card (*n*): also known as a picture card (a Jack, Queen, or King).

---

fifth street (*n*): the fifth and final card in a board game, also known as **the river** in Hold Em.

---

fish (*n*): a player known as a consistent loser.

45. Perception is reality

Poker is the game closest to the Western conception of life, where life and thought are recognized as intimately combined, where free will prevails over philosophies of fate or of chance, where men are considered moral agents and where—at least in the short run—the important thing is not what happens but what people think happens. —John Luckacs, author, *Poker and the American Character*

I mage isn't everything, but it usually counts for plenty. In terms of table image, the adjectives tight, loose, good, or poor become almost quantifiable when applied to a player's chances to succeed at a bluff. All things being equal, a tight, conservative "rock" (who rarely bluffs) has better bluffing odds than a loose, hyper-aggressive type that bets on anything. On a given night, however, images can be somewhat altered by success or failure. If you're raking in every other pot, your "image" is considered good; other players tend to give you more respect and will probably be less inclined to call your bluff or semibluff. On the other hand, if you're known as someone who rarely folds (and usually loses), you should have no shortage of takers when you bet/bluff.

♦   ♦   ♦

A bluff is likelier to succeed when:
- you're known as a tight player;
- you're in a game with fairly tight players;
- your image is burnished by a spate of good fortune;
- you play your bluffing hand the same exact way as you play your winning hand(s);
- you're in late position;
- you're in late position, and everyone else has checked;
- there are few (no more than two) other players left in the hand;
- the stakes are significant enough to make it "hurt" to call;
- you can successfully (mis)represent a particular hand based on "scare" tactics, in which you bet or raise on a scare card, typically something that appears intimidating (you bet on the ace as if it paired you up or bet another card in a series of numbers for the straight, etc.).

A bluff is less likely to succeed when:
- you're in a game with mostly loose players;
- you bet big and tell your opponents to "save your money" (if you're genuinely interested in their financial portfolio, your wouldn't be playing poker with them; there are no guaranteed talking tells, but if there were, this would be at the top of the list);
- you bluff too frequently;.
- the stakes are too low;
- more than two players are still in the hand;

- more than two players are still in the hand;
- the pot is huge;
- patterns emerge—like Stinky's criteria for the old college try: He will always try to steal a pot on the river against one other player (whoever you are, call him);
- you've recently been caught in a bluff (build up your table image before trying again);
- you're head to head with a loose, lousy player.

Pokerese

flop (*v* or *n*): the first three community cards simultaneously displayed on the board in games such as Texas Hold Em and Omaha.

flushing (*v*): when a player is drawing cards in the hopes of pulling a flush.

fold out of turn (*v. phrase*): when a player folds before his or her turn. This is technically against the rules of Poker and looked down upon in any serious game.

46. You can sooner bluff out a good (tight) player than a lousy (loose) one

Poker without money, in our opinion, is like an ice cream cone without the ice cream, Paris without a double bed, Tom Wolfe without the vernacular. —Joyce Wadler, writer, *The New York Times*

I t is often thus: The good die young; justice takes a holiday; the turtle beats the hare. They're not precisely oxymorons. Maybe they're conundrums. Or simple contradictions. Perhaps irony?

Whatever.

♥　♥　♥

These adages are more proof—if it's affirmation you seek—of fate's twisted sense of humor. In a poker context, good players are usually easier to bluff out because:

- lousy players are blind to the subtle subterfuge and setup that any smart bluff needs;
- lousy players are more interested in retaining their "manhood" (or womanhood) than their money;
- lousy players would sooner let you have their mothers for a weekend (what is it about poker players and their mothers?) than face the possibility that they may have folded a winning hand;
- as much as they love to bluff, lousy players love even more to catch someone in a bluff;
- lousy players will more often call with weak hands;
- lousy players don't realize how much money they're losing by always keeping someone "honest."

And because the strongest, most secure, players don't like to get bluffed out more than anyone else, but they (we) know that it is part of the game. On occasion, it's no big deal.

47. Even better, semibluff

The semibluff is one of the least understood tools of poker, yet it is a very valuable and potent weapon. —David Sklansky, author, *The Theory of Poker*

The concept of hedging your bet(s) has been around for ages, but David Sklansky is often credited with giving it a name, and a specific spin, in poker terms. He defines it as "a bet with a hand, which if called, does not figure to be the best hand at the moment but has a reasonable chance of outdrawing those hands that initially called it. . . . When you bet as a semibluff, you are rooting to win right there just as you are when you make a pure bluff. . . . However, in contrast to a pure bluff, your hand must have some chances of improving to the best hand."

Basically you're doubling your chances to win, which is always a good play.

♣   ♣   ♣

48. It pays to advertise (or does it?)

A good player will at times purposely play poorly to vary his game.
—William J. Florence

There is no shortage of schools—and schoolmasters—when it comes to the promise of a complete poker education. Alas, there are campuses built solely on a foundation of bluffs.

A popular university of thought revolves around the "advertising" principle. That is: You don't always bluff to win; you bluff to get caught, thereby demonstrating a willingness to bluff, thereby you're more likely to be called when you've got the goods, thereby . . .

Wrong.

This teacher believes you'll get called often enough—about 50 percent of the time, my colleagues instruct—so why play for the loss.

Bluff because you have a chance to steal the pot. Bluff for one reason: to win.

♠   ♠   ♠

49. Online play is off

These online guys have no table manners. —Norman Chad, television and World Series of Poker color commentator

It's not poker exactly. It's virtual poker.

Agreed, it's probably helpful for novices learning the game. And I suppose there are enough pigeons with itchy claws on their mouse to warrant a periodic foray into cyberspatial relations. But don't be fooled into believing that online poker is the real deal (I promise, that's the last usage of the played-out phrase). It ain't real if you can't look into an opponent's eyes—or sunglasses. It ain't authentic if you can't smell the fetid breath of fear in the air. It ain't the genuine article if you can't lay down cash or chips.

♦ ♦ ♦

Internet play has some other specific differences that you need to know before you type in your credit card number. For one, there's much more bluffing online; it's harder to be deceptive when you're up against live competition. (Again, you avoid the fear factor that only comes from committing your chips and having to wait neutrally, coldly, interminably for someone to decide when, or if, to call. Plus, it's also easier to call—just a click away.) Secondly, and perhaps most importantly, subtle, highly strategic moves are usually wasted on cyberplayers because they're often subdividing their attention on cell phones, television, or catching up on their e-mail. And: You don't play with the same people often enough to catch nuances such as table image. However, one tell is easy to read: the speed in which they bet. Here, "slow play" has a more literal meaning: The greater the delay in betting (usually), the poorer the hand.

It's the lack of observational certainty that makes stone-cold reality buffs uneasy about this sort of virtual environment.

Pokerese

fourth Street (*n*): the fourth community card in a board game, also known in Hold 'Em as **the turn**. In stud, it's merely the fourth card dealt to each player.

50. Act like you've been there before

> When you get into the end zone, act like you've been there before.
> —attributed to both Tom Landry and Vince Lombardi, Hall of Fame
> football coaches

Talk about the prototypical old-school vs. new-school debate:
- Jerry Rice vs. Terrell Owens;
- Ray Scott vs. Stuart Scott;
- WPIX (local high school football) vs. Time-Warner, Inc. (America Online, Inc. Advertising.com, Inc. America Online Latin America, Inc. AOL (UK) Ltd. AOL Web Access Group CompuServe Interactive Services, Inc. Mailblocks, Inc. MapQuest.com, Inc. Moviefone, Inc. Singingfish, Inc. BlackVoices.com, Inc. Courtroom Television Network LLC Home Box Office, Inc. HBO Films MovieTickets.com, Inc. New Line Cinema Corporation Fine Line Features Time Inc.

IPC Group Limited Southern Progress Corporation Synapse Group, Inc. Time Warner Book Group Inc. Time Warner Book Group UK Time4 Media, Inc. Time Warner Cable Road Runner LLC Time Warner Telecom Inc. Turner Broadcasting System, Inc. The Cartoon Network CNN News Group TBS Inc. International Turner Sports, Inc. Atlanta National League Baseball Club, Inc. The WB Television Network Warner Bros. Entertainment Inc. Castle Rock Entertainment, Inc. DC Comics Inc. Vertigo Comics WildStorm Productions Movielink, LLC Warner Bros. Television Warner Independent Pictures).

After the most spectacular, tackle-missing, jock-juking, crazy-legged touchdown runs, the great ones (Jim Brown through Barry Sanders) would flip or hand the ball to the nearest official and jog to the side-line. They acted like they'd been there before because they had been—many, many times. No fuss, no muss. No spiking, no shuffling, no phoning, no autographing, no taunting. No bullshit.

But jaw-dropping moves didn't move product like yap-flapping media manipulation. Skill and talent were no longer sufficient. Personality became king. Blame mega-moguls, meta-bucks, and/or marketing mavens. Blame the damned National Football League for penalizing the perpetrators, thereby turning rabble-rousing punks into fan-friendly rebels. Blame SportsCenter. Blame Muhammad Ali (who begat Broadway Joe Namath and Neon Deion Sanders, not to mention one-hit wonders like Icky Woods and the Boz). There was a simple formula for self-promotion: ink + highlight coverage = high Q ratings and the postcareer good life.

And what does this have to do with poker?

The most old school of pastimes has, for better and worse, become new school. The bright lights are in the process of overexposing a heretofore hidden (or at least uncovered) treasure. More ink and more cameras equal more and bigger assholes . . . er, personalities. Colorful characters such as Amarillo Slim, Doyle Brunson, Nick the Greek, and Puggy Pierson have begotten mouthy, posturing bores like Phil Hellmuth, Jr., Men Nguyen, Ellix Powers, and Patty Gallagher.

Poker is not, nor should it be, a passionless, colorless, character-less game; there's too much at stake: money and reputation, perhaps foremost. Miraculous suck-out victories and tragic suck-out beats will always engender a response, good and bad, classy and tacky. But within those emotional highs and lows lie an honorable code of conduct and tradition to uphold. Without that, it's not much more than professional wrestling.

Lose the bad acting, boys and girls. Or, at the least, act like you've been there before.

Pokerese

freezeout (*n*): a tournament that has no re-buys; which means: once your chips are gone, you're out (also called a **shootout**).

51. Fight fire with . . . less fire

You can shear a sheep many times, but you can only skin him once. —Amarillo Slim

When confronted with a super aggressive opponent (and if that's not your natural style), it doesn't pay for you to stay toe to toe trading shots. Feint. Jab. Rope the dope.

♥ ♥ ♥

If Mr. or Ms. Testosterone try to control the action with their bang-bang (bet-raise) play, let them. Or let them think they are. One way to take some sting out of their furious flurries is to continuously check and call (this tactic is most effective when they're seated to your left and you've got the goods). Let them dictate the action. Let them mistake your silence for weakness. Let them think they can bluff and bully you around. Then: big-bang-boom. You quietly lay down your cards and scoop up the pot they so helpfully built up for you.

Your play will likely drive them bonkers and, if they don't wise up or chill out, broke.

Pokerese

grind (*v*): to play tight (usually, but not always, in a low-limit game) and accept relatively small winnings.

---

grinder (*n*): a player who *consistently* wins smaller amounts.

52. There's gamesmanship in all games

The American team has 11 nice guys. And Paul Azinger.
—Seve Ballesteros, professional golfer

Within the rules of most games, it's entirely appropriate—make that imperative—to take advantage of each and every competitive edge that can tilt the odds in your favor.

♣   ♣   ♣

Take golf, the so-called gentleman's game, in which the honor system is still honored. You're supposed to call potentially tournament-losing penalties on yourself, even if no one else notices. Yet, in the crucible of competition . . . well, crap happens. During the 1989 Ryder Cup match (the United States versus Europe for worldwide bragging rights), American Paul Azinger refused Spaniard Seve Ballesteros's request to change a scuffed ball. For the next three Cups (that's six years of grudge-holding), the two pros battled and baited each other with the pettiest of complaints: "standing too close ... jiggling pocketed coins while opponent putted ... coughing ... illegal drop ... and even, reportedly, "caddy flatulence." Broadcasters justified the heated exchanges by talking up the intense pressure of the venerable Cup. ("Pressure?" golfer Lee Trevino famously said when asked if he felt any on the final hole of a major, standing over a putt that meant, say, the difference between $1 million first prize and $500,000 for second. "You don't know what pressure is until you play for five dollars a hole with only two in your pocket."

There's a finely arguable line in every pastime and/or activity that separates juvies from gentlemen; cutthroat cheats from harmless prevaricators; and classless, boorish gamesmanship from heated, bearish gamesmanship. (Some would contend that any gamesmanship is allowable as long as it remains within the bounds of sportsmanship. But, then again, no one—except ESPN shills—ever called poker a sport.)

Where and how is that line drawn? And who draws it?

You do.

53. Everything is a game

Be happy while you're living, for you're a long time dead.
—Scottish Proverb

It's not all fun and games. But, then again, it's not necessarily life or death. (Actually it is, but there's little benefit dwelling on it in those terms.)

Loosen up. Relax. Release stress and pressure (which are entirely manmade; if you choose not to feel them, they no longer exist). Approach it (life) as one long-lasting diversion, and take each day as it comes—as just another 24-hour session.

◆ ◆ ◆

- There'll be another one tomorrow;
- Some rules are always applicable;
- Show up on time;
- Work hard;
- Play hard;
- Keep score;

- Have fun;
- No one gets out alive;
- Take it seriously, but not solemnly.

Pokerese

head to head or **heads up** (*n. phrase*): when only two players are vying for a pot.

high low or **hi-lo** (*n* or *adj*): a form of poker in which the best hand splits with the "worst." Some games you need an 8-low or better to qualify for the low hand.

54. The house rules

A man's trust is a valuable thing, Button. You don't want to lose it for a handful of cards. —Robert Duvall, actor, as Bluebonnet "Boss" Spearmint in *Open Range*

The rules of most games are codified; however, their code of ethics is an amorphous, shifty lot. For example, a civilized society dictates that it is a gross violation of individual privacy if you peek (without a warrant) into your neighbor's personal effects. Yet where is it written, for example, that you cannot peek at your neighbor's cards? And herein is the ethical dilemma: If you can, should you?

There's no Hoyle on definitive poker behavior, but there are house rules. And different houses have different directives, often diametrically opposed, on almost everything: You can check and raise; no check-raising allowed . . . three-raise maximum; unlimited raising . . . no credit accepted; only checks allowed (some high rollers, afraid of the game being rolled, don't want any cash around).

Be they arbitrary or revolutionary, one commandment trumps all: What the house says, goes. If you wish to change or modify an edict, petition the house. If you can't live with the outcome, buy your own house; make your own rules.

Pokerese

hit and run (*v. phrase*): when a winning player voluntarily leaves a game after an especially short duration of play.

Hold 'Em (*n*): shortened (interchangeable) name for Texas Hold 'Em.

55. Always lie, never cheat

Everythin' over on this side is wrong and everythin' on this side is right. This is anything in life, doesn't matter what it is. The closer you can stay to this line, the more successful you're gonna be.
—"Pug" Pierson

There are some powers greater than "the house," and they reside within each individual. Here is my line—and ethical compass—in poker:

◆   ◆   ◆

Lying is part of the game, maybe the greatest part. Even Mr. William J. Florence, who got so much wrong in *The Gentlemen's Handbook on Poker*, acknowledged that "a player who never bluffs at poker is not in sympathy with the game." If you never lie about your cards, your opponents will have your number: 0 (as in the amount of money you can reasonably expect to make over the long haul). There is even an entire gray area (see No. 56) in which you and your conscience must be the final arbiters.

But *cheating* (which, like pornograhy, may be difficult to precisely define, but you know it when you see it)—no way, no how—is non-negotiable. It is an unforgivable offense, a venial, cardinal, and ordinal sin against God, nature and, especially, man.

Pokerese

hole cards (*n*): in stud, they're synonymous with down or unexposed cards. (In Hold 'Em, they're also referred to as pocket cards.)

HORSE (*n*): a game, usually held as a tournament event, in which five different variations are played (one per rotation or round): Hold Em; Omaha; Razz; Seven-Card Stud; Eights or Better.

56. You know it when you see it (but you don't always get a good look)

My friend, if the queen of spades is not under your hand, I owe you an apology. —Anonymous player (circa late 19th Century), after literally pinning an opponent's hand to the table with a bowie knife

What exactly is cheating?

♣ ♣ ♣

There is no gray, for example, in *Card manipulation*: A good card mechanic—like a skilled sleight-of-hand artist—is almost impossible to detect. He can effortlessly grab a quick peek at the top or bottom card and keep track of who gets it (or second deal it, after everyone else gets a card, for himself) simply by shifting his grip on a deck. He can also false shuffle—always keeping the bottom card at the bottom of the deck; or moving the bottom card to the top; or leaving the top card or cards undisturbed at the top; or even stacking the deck for himself or a confederate with a specific hand. He can palm a card—secreting it into his shirt or pants pocket, or under his shirtsleeve—and bring it into play when needed, or hold it out for the next hand if no one notices the deck is light. He can even shift the cut, returning the deck to its original order; or, more insidiously, perform "the step," in which the cut cards are seemingly squared with the rest of the deck but actually stick out sufficiently so that (with one quick move or step) the bottom pile is placed back at the bottom. (Often a small ledge is put into the deck by one cheater so that his co-conspirators can cut it at the precise location; this is also referred to as a jog or a needle.)

Collusion: Even more difficult to detect, this scam includes any form of cooperation between two or more players who intend to share the profits after the game. They may use gestures or table talk as signals to indicate their respective hands (or their opponents'); initiate or calibrate betting patterns; or divert attention during card manipulation.

Card marking: Cheaters may use a professionally predoctored deck, in which the markings are seen by special "x-ray" glasses, or there may be subtle design differences perceptible only to those looking for them. More often, the alterations are done on the spot—by literally scratching the surface (thumbnailing); or by bending, folding, or crimping the corner of a card; or, much more sophisticatedly, daubing the back of a card with special ink (again, visible with special specs sold in novelty stores or magic shops).

57. Catch the anglers

Not the way I play it, no. —W.C. Fields, actor, in *My Little Chickadee* (replying to the question: "Is this a game of chance?")

"**S**hooting the angle" covers crimes much more heinous (even if some permissive houses may allow them) than just *playing* an angle. If not outright cheaters, angle shooters are antithetical to the spirit of the game. They go well beyond the ethical and moral limits of trying to gain a legitimate edge. They're off the edge with their weaselly little acts of commission, which include (in ascending order of weaselness):

♠   ♠   ♠

Fake (or string) betting: An angle shooter makes a play—maybe an unspoken gesture towards his chips, or, worse, picks them up and starts to move them into the pot—but stops when he notes another player preparing to call. He checks instead, and is saved a bet or call he did not want to make, or he gets a free look at how his bluff might play. Either way, it's a dubious "angle." Is it cheating or skirting the edge of the code? It's your call, but in my book (this one), it is, at the least, aggravated malfeasance (perhaps even justifying an Old West-style "attitude adjustment").

Misdeclaring or misrepresenting hands: On the laydown, someone says "I have a straight"—to which your natural instinct is to toss two pair into the discards—only to hear: "Oh, golly, I thought I had a straight; I guess I misread that last card." If you've already mucked your cards, your hand is dead; and, if no other players remain to call his busted straight, he will steal the pot (not with legitimate poker-playing strategy, but with pretty-close-to-outright theft). In the old days, he might have gotten shot or maybe just had his trigger hand bloodied. Today he sits there and, if house rules permit, gathers in his ill-gotten gains.

Money manipulating (aka "too many hands in the pot"): In most friendly house games, players make their own change—throwing in, say, a hundred-dollar bill on a $60 bet and taking out two twenties in exchange. With the "light-fingered discount"—which is straight-up stealing—they may put in a tenspot (all the while giving the verbal cue, "here's my C-note . . . and taking $40") for a nifty gross profit of $130.

58. Take the smell test

The best protection against poker cheats is the knowledge of how they operate and some ability at recognizing their slick sleight of hand and other crooked ruses. —John Scarne, author, *Guide to Modern Poker*

Sniff around. If something seems fishy, it probably is (assuming you have the "normal" levels of paranoia and skepticism any good player needs).

In a situation where you've played with the same people for a long time, doubts tend to fall on the newest members: Who brought him into the game? What do you know about him? Do you think he's responsible for some of the recent hinky goings-on ? What *has* been going on?

- Cards have often been found on the floor, seemingly crimped;
- Several pots have appeared shy at the end;
- And Doc has gotten hammered with several really bad beats.

Something or someone has been spoiling the long-term game's

grade-A bonhomie and comfort zone, and the investigation inevitably follows the taint of new meat.

Humans are generally fearful of outsiders. Countries have a word for it—xenophobia—and it often fuels those anti-immigration initiatives. And citizens of Poker Nation, by dint of their national pastime, are probably more mistrustful, wary, leery, and skeptical of others than most. Besides nobody wants his/her utopian setup threatened in any way, and if there's a weasel in the fox house, let's catch him and cook him.

Some house games have gotten so draconian—no new players; no strangers; no one we can't beat like a drum—they're becoming like casinos. Besides, where's the fun in that? Never play with strangers? So how do you replenish players after they've moved on (to the next world or otherwise)? Not to get too sentimental about this subject, but weren't all of your friends strangers at some point? And what about true-blue companions who change their colors over time?

We had a founding member of the Wednesday Night Game who'd been playing without incident for 15 years until he began "interacting" fishily with several pots a night. He rarely shortchanged the pot more than a sawbuck; we pointed it out, and he apologized profusely for his honest mistake. He was so liked by most of the regulars that we didn't really want to acknowledge that he—and we—obviously had a problem. What caused him to resort to petty thievery? Pressure from the wife? Reversing business fortunes? Never knew. Never cared. (Not everyone in the game thought his behavior unusual and they refused to consider that Jeff—oops, no names—would stoop to cribbing a couple of extra bucks from his poker pals.) I was content to watch him like a hawk, especially when I was involved in the action. Then, one day, he stopped. No more pot filching. No more suspect moves with money. It's been a while, and he remains a regular. He and his fingers have stayed clean. We never talked about it; he would've only denied it. I used to like and trust the guy. Not anymore. But I'll be glad to take his money. Unless he goes on another spree. Then we're going to have words. Lots of them.

♦   ♦   ♦

Other than catching a cheat in the act, suspicious behavior includes:

An exchange of signals between two (or more) players—manifest in unusual gestures or glances, or consistent spoken expressions.

Sloppy dealing by inexperienced card manipulators who make frequent mistakes or who hold the cards in unusual or unnatural ways. Also, listen carefully: When a cheat is second dealing or bottom dealing, there's a sound a card makes—it's been described as a "swish-click"—when it's being pulled from between two other cards.

Cards discovered in unlikely places—underneath the table; in the bathroom; in someone's pocket.

On occasion, excessively suspicious minds will feed on each other, propelling them to turn a convergence of coincidental occurrences into a full-blown cheating scandal. Make sure you're sure before you accuse anyone of cheating. Your game will never be the same.

59. Counter con men

Trust everybody, but cut the cards. —Finley Peter Dunne, author,
Mr. Dooley in Peace and in War

I f, say, six months after suspicions are first aroused, and your stomach is still in knots trying to figure out if you're being cheated, reread and heed principle No. 58. If you feel cheated, you probably have been. But, even without absolute proof, you can take some specific steps that will, at minimum, make the rounders sweat and (because sweating and "easy money" are diametrically opposed) soon look for easier marks.

♥   ♥   ♥

ANGLE/CON/SCAM

Fake Betting: Wait until every player has completed his/her action. If he/she seems to be stalling, feigning, or preparing to shoot some angle, put the dawdler on the spot by asking "Are you making a play?" before making yours.

Misdeclaration: Always check (and double-check if it belongs to a suspect) the "winning" hand before throwing yours away.

Money manipulation: Watch everyone with a hand in the pot, especially individuals who've made more than one "honest" mistake. Disallow quick moves—in and out. (You want to facilitate fast play, but you don't want players who're a little too fast.)

Card manipulation: Always cut the cards, and make sure there's no further shuffling. In games, or situations, where cards are being dealt face up, there's no need for the deck to be held in anyone's hand (it should remain on the table); make it a house rule. Note any unusual hand positions used by a dealer. (Two popular versions of the "mechanic's grip" are: 1. moving the index and middle fingers from the long side of the deck to the short side; or 2. holding the deck with the thumb on top, index finger around the front edge, middle and ring fingers underneath, and little finger on the rear edge.)

PREVENTION/PROTECTION

Swap (that's swap, not swab) decks often: Ideally you want to rotate two decks and change them as needed (at least once a night).

Scrutinize cards often—by eyeball and touch: You won't be able to see invisible daubs without special specs (or super powers, in which case your advantages are insurmountable), but you can discern crimping, shading, and even design differences. And observe if other players seem too interested in the backs of cards (not as policemen but as con men).

Recount the cards: If a full accounting is not tenable because of trust or speed issues, you can occasionally rely on a "stub" count; when all seven players are in for a full hand of seven-card stud, there should be three cards left (or "in the stub"). Obviously there are very few opportunities for this type of remedy.

Use shoes: These (usually) plastic containers—which are compulsory in casinos at baccarat and blackjack (though not always at poker)—enable cards to be slid out one at a time from one or more decks. You rarely, if ever, see them in home games because they're so unfriendly, untrusting, uncheap, and unquick. (You're continuously passing the one-deck shoe around to each dealer, who then must reshuffle and refill.) The shoe is a next-to-last resort in your fight against angle shooters, scammers, rounders, con men, and cheaters.

The last resort? You cash in and walk away.

Pokerese

house (*n*): any establishment (from a private home to a casino) that runs a game.

60. Nowhere to run, nowhere to hide

Poker does not test character—it defines it. —Lou Krieger, writer, *The New York Times Magazine*

Man conceals; poker reveals.

If you're an insecure jerk (no matter how much you try to camouflage that fact), eventually your elemental disposition will emerge. Competition, stress, tension, crises—they all tend to weaken defenses and display a human's true nature. Sometimes it's not a pretty sight; sometimes it's prettier than anyone else—even you—ever imagined.

♣   ♣   ♣

Poker's compressed, heightened reality will accelerate and accentuate the "exposure" process. In just a few hours' time, you can pretty much devise, administer, and grade many of life's greatest tests.

You pass or you fail.

61. Take stock

It's hard work...playing poker. Don't let anyone tell you different. —Stu Ungar

You need few hard goods:
  • legal tender;
  • clothes (optional);
  • deck of cards;
  • opponents.

But at the end of every session, you should run through your inventory. Determine if there's anything valuable missing and what can be done to replenish it. Take detailed notes.

How well did you adhere to your game plan?

What, if anything, caused you to deviate?

How well were you able to make the necessary adjustments?

Was your bankroll sufficient?

Evaluate your progress or regression. (Determine if you should move up or down in stakes.)

Keep a ledger of every player's wins and losses (your own included), tracking noticeable changes (+ and -).

Mark down any new tells—theirs and yours—as well as specific game variations in which you did best and worst.

Periodically update and distill your notations. Study them before each session. Every six months, file them away and start anew. If this strikes you as too much like work, you're right.

♥   ♥   ♥

Pokerese

Indian Poker or **Schmuck** (*n*): a stud variation that is only played in a home game late at night preferably with alcohol (or an equivalent recreational substance) at hand; every player is dealt one down card, which is then shown to everyone but himself (this is usually accomplished by placing said card on each player's forehead). There is one round of betting; high card wins.

62. Do your homework

It will not always be summer. Build barns. —Hesiod, 8th-century (B.C.) Greek poet, *Theogony, Works and Days*

Right now, someone somewhere is putting in the extra time and effort. She may be getting up at 5 A.M. to practice with her coach before making it to middle school; or she may be online, diligently poring through the bloggers for some esoteric but effective tips; or she may be laying out sample hands while reading Doyle Brunson's *Super System*.

♠ ♠ ♠

What are you doing to keep up? Oh, yeah, you're reading this book. Smart, forward thinking. Keep up the good work. Keep practicing, poring, and reading. It *will* all pay off.

63. Nobody wants to hear your sad stories

As an expert of poker and as an aficionado, I don't discuss my bad beats. It's boring. —Vince Van Patten

E xactly. Who wants to hear someone—anyone—go on and on about the huge, ferocious fish that got away after a 90-minute struggle; the pure 195-yard bunker shot that landed inches from the cup; or the camel trip to Upper Golgotha, from which your neighbor will be showing her 600 slides and offering a "fascinating" three-hour commentary (scheduled on the evening of the first World Series game . . . and yes, your wife has already accepted the invitation before you were even consulted).

But you don't have to be a bad, or selfish, person to feel little or no interest in what are obviously important events in your friends' lives. You weren't there. No matter how deft a storyteller these people are, you have no palpable frame of reference. You're simply lost in a haze of minutiae. You try to be supportive, but any enthusiasm is feigned.

Still and all, there are aficionados who enjoy hearing about some-body else's bad beat. (The editor of this book, for example, says he can't get enough hard-luck stories; he claims to derive a vicarious pleasure and some benefit in the cautionary tales of others.)

♠   ♠   ♠

Fine. Here's mine:

Many years ago—in five-card draw, pot limit, with five players—I was dealt three aces. To my right, Lucky (short for Luckman) bet $15. I raised $15, and Rich bumped us $20. The other two guys at the table folded, and Lucky and I both called. With each man's $5 ante, the pot stood at $175. Lucky drew one card, as did I—faking the two pair; Rich, a wealthy man who bet for the sheer fun of it, asked for three cards. After the draw, Lucky bet $77. With three aces going in, I didn't even look at my last card when I said, "Raise a hundred." Without a pause, Rich raised another hundred.

Were both Lucky and I to call, the pot would exceed $1,000 ($1,006, to be exact). This was a milestone our game had yet to reach. We had just begun to play pot limit, in which the total amount in the pot could be bet at any time.

Lucky didn't look happy; in fact, he appeared so downright mis-erable that I was starting to worry. What, me worry? With the hand I had? Yep, even with four aces. That's right; on a one-card draw, I pulled the case bullet. So, I was feeling mighty powerful until Lucky began looking so lousy.

I had been playing poker with Luckman since college, and I knew all of his tells. Mostly Lucky's a bad actor; he pretends to have garbage—which he sells with different faces of bewilderment, even pain—and then bets the limit. Glancing at the huge pile of bills and chips, with the most lamentable look I have ever seen at a poker table, he simply said: "Pot."

What?

"I'll bet the pot," Lucky said.

There I sat, in the biggest hand of my poker-playing life with a virtual lock of four aces, and I'm thinking: I could lose. I knew he didn't have a royal flush (I had all the aces); maybe he had four kings. I had three choices: fold, call. or raise.

"I call," I said.

Rich realized this was one pot he was not going to steal; he folded.

"Lucky," I said, "there's only one hand that beats me." He had it: a straight flush to the jack. In five-card draw. There was a collective gasp at the table. This was out of a bad movie. I certainly thought it could happen, but I couldn't believe it actually did happen—to me. Lucky looked almost genuinely pained when he said: "Tough burn."

Years before, at college, after a particularly bad run of hands or an especially bad burn, I would fling my cards across the table or stomp around angrily. That was then. Now I took it like a man. Maybe these are just the sort of moments that make a boy grow up, that allow him perhaps his first glimpse of an impassive, unforgiving, and unhelpful world.

Anyway, that's my story.

64. It's a marathon, not a sprint

Poker is a combination of luck and skill. People think mastering the skill part is hard, but they're wrong. The trick to poker is mastering the luck. That's philosophy. Understanding luck is philosophy, and there are some people who aren't ever gonna fade it. That's what sets poker apart. And that's what keeps everyone coming back for more. —Jesse May, author, *Shut Up and Deal*

Think of poker as one very, very, long game. Trends will come and go. Streaks will run their course. Losers will lose; winners will win.

Each session is an incremental step in a vast, incredible process. You never stop moving forward. You never stop learning. Each time out, your job is to maximize winnings, minimize losses. You don't look back other than to savor your triumphs (briefly) and/or figure out how to improve your play.

♣   ♣   ♣

Tomorrow is another day. And another. Pace yourself. And another. And another.

Pokerese
jack it up (*v. phrase*): slang for *raise*.
joker (*n*): a card (or two) that comes in every deck (but should never be used).
judith (*n*): the queen of hearts
juice (*n*): 1. marking on the cards, put there by a cheat. 2. the percentage of each pot that is kept by the house.

65. Lucky in cards, unlucky in love

If you sacrifice poker for girls, don't expect them to show up. They'll only show up for a man who wouldn't dream of sacrificing poker for girls. —John Huston, movie director, *The Maltese Falcon*

"Okay, well, fine, and good," your non-poker mates say. "You've proven yourself to be a ruthless, cold, and calculating master at the game. How can you be possibly trusted in a personal or even a professional relationship?"

Fair question

Very reasonable.

No easy answers.

That's it?

Well, on the face of it, the acknowledged poker traits—riddled with lying, bullying, controlling, dominating, misdirecting, and manipulating—have little in common with the gentler, more loving, sensitive, considerate, loyal, honest, and steadfast qualities that are essential to attracting and sustaining all healthy, mutually respectful bonds of affection and even love. But . . .

[You'll need a helluva humonguous "but" to make this case.]

It's a yin and yang thing.

Not bupkis up the yin-yang again?

No, this is a different usage entirely. It refers to the multi- (or at least dual-) sided aspects of a person's fundamental nature. Few of us are simply this or that. We're this, that, and other things. We are rarely One Thing or Another. We're complex characters—Strong and Weak; Kind and Self-driven; In and Out; Up and Down; Have and Have Not.

Where's the yin-yang connection?

From birth to death, men and women strive to compartmentalize and integrate our finest, most useful qualities with some of our less noble but equally useful and useable characteristics. We follow at least two connective, occasionally divergent paths: 1. yin ("the feminine passive principle in nature that in Chinese cosmology is exhibited in darkness, cold or wetness" that combines with 2. yang ("the masculine active principle in nature that in Chinese cosmology is exhibited in light, heat or dryness") to produce all that comes to be.

We can be both a cold-blooded killer at the card table and a warm, generous and gentle relative, neighbor, friend or lover. We are mutually inclusive.

♠   ♠   ♠

For what it's worth, a relationship is somewhat analogous to poker: Neither is an exact science; both rely on psychology, mathematics, money management, probability, resilience, and a little bit of good fortune.

66. Poker is like sex, and vice versa

There is a rhythm of tension-discharge, which is constantly repeated. At the beginning of play it is quiet, gradually there is a crescendo of excitement until a peak is reached, and finally there is a period of quiet. —Ralph Greening, psychoanalyst

There's the thrill of the chase.

There are the great expectations every time you decide to play the game.

There is a different rhythm in every encounter.

There are the series of tensions building up to a satisfying conclusion (on a good night). Pleasurable rewards await the intuitive, patient, and creative player.

There is skill involved, but it's often a gamble, too.

Winning increases libido; losing depresses it.

Sometimes you get screwed royally.

♦   ♦   ♦

In the end, only you can decide whether you're in it for a one-night stand or a lifelong love affair.

Pokerese

kibitz (*v*): 1. to observe and comment on the action as a non-player; (less frequent usage) 2. to observe and comment on the action while playing.

kibitzer (*n*): one who observes or comments on the action (either as a player or non-player).

kick (*v*): another term for "raise", preferred term of more experienced poker players (as opposed to "bump").

67. Know (and follow) the rules

There are few things that are so unpardonably neglected in our country as poker.... Now and then you find ambassadors who have sort of a general knowledge of the game, but the ignorance of the people is fearful. Why, I have known clergymen, good men, kind-hearted, liberal, sincere, and all that, who did not know the meaning of a "flush." It is enough to make one ashamed of one's species. —Mark Twain, author, *The Adventures of Tom Sawyer*

Every house and home has its own rules, its own games, and its own etiquette. Know them all. If possible, learn (about) them before you sit down. It's quite irritating to have the same stooge ask the same players for the same clarification or explanation of the same variation again and again and again and again. But even more bothersome are players that don't/won't ask. In their obstinate ignorance (one of the worst combinations in any arena), they stumble and flail around—slowing play to a tortuous crawl, wondering whether to fold or call (and usually doing it out of turn), inciting opponents to a brawl. (Maybe that's their ingenious strategy: to throw everyone else on tilt.)

♣   ♣   ♣

Few amounts of money are worth winning if you have to endure these doofuses. All venues should post their house rules, and No. 1 should be: No Obstinate, Ignorant Doofuses Allowed.

Pokerese

kicker (*n*): 1. in any hand, the high card that accompanies a pair (or two pair), occasionally used to determine a winner (if, say, two players each have a pair of tens, the pot goes to whomever has the highest kicker); 2. in draw, denotes the high card (usually ace or king) kept in the hopes of pairing up.

68. Take control

When the good player achieves self-control through discipline and understands his opponents through thinking, he then can seize control of the game. —Frank R. Wallace

The key to control—gaining it, holding onto it, expanding it—is in your ability to master emotions, circumstances, and people.

♣   ♣   ♣

Emotions: You don't want to become too high or too low, win or lose. Getting caught up in the hype and hoopla is, in the end, a sucker's game. Keep your mind free and clear of any residual emotions—anger, envy, even joy—that can divert attention from your game plan.

Circumstances: This is probably the toughest of the three areas to manage and regulate because, by definition, exigent conditions are beyond your control. You can, however, predict with some accuracy their likely patterns.

People: If you've done your homework, know the players inside and out, and have the charm and force of personality to influence their decision-making (and the salesmanship to close the deal), you can greatly influence—and, to some degree, hold sway over—the thoughts and behavior of small to large groups. It will probably surprise you to discover how easily and happily some people will cede control over huge chunks of their lives to charismatic individuals who seem to know what they're doing.

Scary, but true. Better you, than them, to have that control.

Pokerese

limit (*adj*): a game that has fixed betting amounts (as opposed to no-limit or pot limit).

limp in (*v. phrase*): in any no-limit game, to just barely call, or call reluctantly. This tactic can be used by a player with a good hand to appear weak.

lineup (*n*): the people playing in a game.

69. Pick the right people

A winner is first and foremost a controller. That's why in life, I'm just a little better than even—and an odds-on favorite to stay that way. —"Pug" Pierson

Only in a perfect world would you have *total* control. Because strong-willed, independent folks, like yourself, cannot be controlled. These are, by and large, not the kind of folks you want to compete against. Yet, in high-stakes house contests or casino tournaments, you can't avoid them. What to do? Play your best and hope the chips fall your way. And work, plan, and dream in the hope of someday finding that utopia.

Having had the pleasure of participating in two extraordinary long-term regular house games, I can confirm: Some control is possible. And: Perfect worlds do exist. But: You're not likely to find, or stumble upon, paradise; you must create it.

To have maximum input—and the opportunity for a maximum return—in any worthwhile startup venture, you should be involved from the start. (If you have some control of the process, you'll have some control of the finished product.) The individuals who organize a weekly night of card playing, for example, can exert a tremendous amount of power over the life of the game. How? In their choice of players, who will of course embody and determine the ultimate life of that game. Just like in the movies, it's all in the casting.

WANTED: undisciplined, ignorant, meek, malleable, filthy rich poker players. Entertaining raconteurs a plus.

♠   ♠   ♠

If you can find three or four players whose resumes are right on the money, you've got yourself a helluva cushy deal. (To hold out for an entire squad of like-minded individuals would be piggish.) Besides, it's no crime to share some of the wealth, and having a couple—no more than two—of worthy (but not superior) opponents should make it more sporting and, in the process, help to sustain your long-term interest.

Pokerese

line work (*n. phrase*): writing (lines, checks, squiggles, etc.) put on a deck by a cheat to mark the cards, so that they can be read during a game.

70. Evaluate personnel periodically (manipulate when necessary)

More players quit poker because of hurt feelings than because of hurt finances. —Frank R. Wallace

Perfect worlds do exist, though rarely forever. And for those stewards who are most vested in perpetuating perfection it may seem like a full-time job.

If you're smart and fortunate enough to construct a dream team, you will be constantly tested by personnel and circumstances—in and out of your control. Taking another page from Mr. Wallace's opportunistic book, you stay on top of your game by becoming, and remaining, *the man*, the one indispensable individual to whom others look for guidance, approval, and conflict resolution. Unlike some other dominions, you don't become the man by strutting, preening, bullying, or nakedly grabbing control from your competitive lessers. Instead, a subtle, delicate, politic—often, a helping—hand is necessary. (When someone runs out of cash, you're the first to offer a loan, providing you know and trust that person; never loan money to anyone you don't know well or who's a known credit risk.)

♥   ♥   ♥

You should be well schooled in the art of the schmooze. When someone loses steadily (and you definitely don't want to lose him entirely), you build up his confidence, you make him feel like an important—nay, an essential—part of the game. You never begrudge him his small victories. In fact, you make a huge show of them. "Wow, Stinky, you played that hand like a master." It's always smart business to praise a competitor who's little competition.

For the good of the game, it's imperative that you get along with disparate, often odious, personalities. If someone makes a biting comment, hold your tongue. Try at all costs to keep tensions to a minimum. Kill them with kindness. Win with class.

You should also be a judicious adjudicator. When disputes arise, you offer a firm but seemingly fair resolution.

Finally, you should be a ruthless eradicator. When novices begin to challenge or even surpass the master, cut them off at the knees without them (or anyone else) discovering your fingerprints on the knife.

Overall, you must be the consummate handler: motivating, manipulating, stroking, intimidating, and—when unavoidable—eliminating the competition.

71. Never stop selling

Aces are larger than life and greater than mountains.
—Mike Caro

A good salesman is always on—catering to his biggest customers while constantly pitching any new business.

♦　　♦　　♦

If it's poker you're promoting, you'll need a complete line of marketing tools, which you can pull out of your sample case at any hour of the day or night (before, during, and after a game):

Customer service: Your in-game salesmanship is primarily devoted to maintaining customer satisfaction and ensuring repeat business. Make sure they're sufficiently content that they'll keep coming back. If you happen to run into a loser from the game in "civilian" life, be friendly and expansive. Tell his mate what a good player he is (never mention how much money he's dropped). Assure him that his luck is bound to change.

Recruitment: You're continuously searching for new bodies—at a party, the corner deli, a pickup basketball game, open school night, open mike night—wherever possible players congregate. At some point during the conversation drop a casual line about poker; see if the bait is bit. Then, subtly mention that you're in a friendly weekly game, that you're always looking for new participants, that you play for "decent" money—mention a dollar figure on the low end of your stakes—where nobody can get hurt too badly. Exchange business cards. If you don't hear from him in a week or so, give him a casual call. Don't appear too eager. Say that there might be an opening, but not immediately.

Hype: The best way to create buzz, to have the hoi polloi clamoring to get in, is to close it to new membership . But make it evident you can get on the "waiting list." During the Golden Era of the Wednesday Night Game, there were nine regulars, but we only allowed eight at the table each week (and, in most seven-card variations, the player to the right of the dealer would sit out that hand); each of us had a number, and when the Wednesday with your number came up and everyone else was in, you sat out . . . way out, at home). If another regular couldn't make it, you of course got the nod; if two regulars bailed, we went to number 10 (or first on the replacement roster). This method not only kept us in eight live bodies every week; it made replenishment seamless when someone dropped out for good. Guys are still trying to get in as regulars after a dozen years on the waiting list.

72. The best man wins

When I was about 6 or 7 my father and I played penny poker. My most notable memory is my grandmother telling me that gambling was unladylike. Now I paint my nails whenever I play to compensate. —Emily Proctor, actress, *CSI: Miami*

And when we say "man," we mean person. Poker is blind to gender/race/class/etc. King, queen, jack o' knaves—it rewards all equally (or unequally) based on skill, bravery, and a bit of help from the gods.

It's not just any game that lets you to test yourself against the world's best. To tee it up with, say, Tiger Woods, you either have to be: 1) a peer professional; 2) a big-time celebrity; or 3) a captain of industry. Suit up, grab a glove and jog out to short at Yankee Stadium, and you'll soon be: 1) tussling with security guards, if not Derek Jeter himself; or 2) wearing pinstripes inside a Bronx jail.

That's the egalitarian beauty of poker. No official hierarchies or handicaps. You need no special equipment to play, only the requisite bucks and a pair of (figurative) cojones. It is a 100-percent meritocracy.

The United States of America, which scores about a 98.7 on the meritocracy scale, has had as its commanders in chief only white Christian men (okay, so mark it down to an 85, still one of the highest percentages in the world of nations) who've been players.

♣   ♣   ♣

Here are a few pertinent Presidential-poker potshots:

"Forget that I'm president of the United States. I'm Warren Harding, playing poker with friends, and I'm going to beat the hell out of them," said Warren G. Harding, the 29th Chief Executive, who played poker twice a week—in or out of the White House.

"Boss, this guy's a pigeon. If you want us to play our best poker for the nation's honor, we'll have this guy's pants before the evening is over. You want us to play customer poker, okay, we can carry him along," said Presidential advisor Harry Vaughan to Harry S Truman (speaking of Winston Churchill during a stateside game). Truman, to use his vernacular, was a helluva player who famously said: "The buck stops here." (The buck was a marker passed around the table to designate the dealer. Originally an actual buck knife was used.) Some historians claim that Truman was picked by Franklin D. Roosevelt as a running mate because he was liked and trusted by Congress members from both parties. He earned that reputation as a regular at Vice President John Nance Garner's poker game, where he became friends with Sam Rayburn, the powerful Speaker of the House.

"When I found officers around me losing more than they could afford,

I stopped playing," said General (later U.S. President) Dwight D. Eisenhower.

"Nick was as good a poker player as, if not better than, anyone we had ever seen. He played a quiet game, but wasn't afraid of taking chances," said James Udall, who served with fellow Navy man, Richard "Nick" Nixon, in the Pacific during WWII. Nixon's political career also got a boost from poker: His winnings (cited as anywhere between "$6,000" and "$10,000") funded a successful campaign for Congress. Just inside the entrance to the Nixon Library and Birthplace in Yorba Linda (CA), framed under glass, is a pair of deuces—the hand with which Lt. Nixon successfully bluffed (and won $1,500).

Pokerese

little blind (*n*): in Texas Hold 'Em, similar to an ante, but actually a forced bet in the first position (to the left of the dealer/button)—half the amount of the Big Blind.

73. Old school beats new school

If I could change anything in the poker world, I'd bar all bad actors from the table. —T.J. Cloutier, professional poker player and World Series of Poker Champion

Best (true) T. J. Cloutier story: He's in Seat 1 at a tournament when the dealer mistakenly sweeps his cards. Cloutier quickly covers the spot where the cards had been and says, "All in." Everyone folds, and T. J. wins the hand without any cards.

That's some impressive playing.

♥   ♥   ♥

It's not just that I'd take Cloutier, Doyle Brunson, and Pug Pierson over Phil Hellmuth, Jr., Men Nguyen, and Patty Gallagher in any Rotisserie Poker league. The true legends (and their peers) would also win hands-down in every Who-Would-You-Rather-Have-A-Beer-With contest (although Nguyen would probably take the How-Many-

Brewskis-Can-You-Hold round). The venerable vets are cinematic, comfortable-in-their-own-skin, dyed-in-the-wool characters, as opposed to made-for-TV, bombastic, synthetic creations.

No doubt this is starting to sound like another rant from a past-his-prime never-was (and so's your mama!) who longingly pines for times he can barely remember. But that doesn't make it any less true.

Just don't get me started on how the sterile, fan-friendly bandwagon has run over the grand ol' game's rugged, raggedy edges . . .

Too late.

Pokerese

lock (*n* or *v*): a certain winner. (See also the **nuts**.)

loose (*adj*): description of a player who's in far too many hands; usually undisciplined, often hyper-aggressive.

74. PG-rated poker is strictly mickey mouse

People were afraid of poker. TV has taken the mystery out of the game. —Lori Keehn, co-owner (with her brother and two sisters) of Saloon No. 10 in Deadwood, SD

There's no sadder sound in all the land than when they "pave paradise and put up a parking lot" (in the words of Joni Mitchell). And the second saddest sound is that of poker's distinctively individualistic terminology being sanitized and diluted into newfangled jargon that seems to have been crafted with Disney-fried blandness. (Is it complete coincidence that ABC-run ESPN televises the World Series of Poker, or just anti-authoritarian, envy-tinged paranoia on my part?)

♠   ♠   ♠

Let's talk "slow play." Since when—and why—does that phrase connote a form of sly, hide-in-the-weeds misdirection? Slow play indicates a table full of retards (no offense) or a bunch of painstakingly deliberate rookies agonizing over every f-f-f-f-r-r-r-r-e-e-e-e-a-a-a-a-a-k-k-k-k-k-i-i-i-i-n-n-n-n-g-g-g-g move. You know what it's called when you low-key your intentions? It's sandbagging, pure and simple.

And "the river"? That's a quaint little description emanating from Texas Hold 'Em, but since when did it become synonymous for all final cards? (I do like *the nuts*, however; that's better than the goods.)

Back in the day, every weekly game had a free hand in the vernacular, creatively spewing and inventing on-the-spot lingo that might then be passed from table to table until it became gospel. Today, you're spoon-fed catchwords and expressions from casino shills and corporate-owned and-sponsored telecasts.

Fuck that.

Pokerese

lowball (*n*): a variation in which the lowest hand (depending on the rules, either ace-2-3-4-5 or (if straights and flushes are disallowed) ace-2-3-4-6.

75. Live by a code

Enjoy every sandwich. —Warren Zevon, singer-songwriter, *Exciteable Boy* (ill with terminal cancer, giving "advice" to David Letterman months before he died)

Some life lessons are learned only at the end.

It would behoove every living human to take a moment, at any age, every once in a while, to borrow or craft an overarching philosophy or an encapsulated code that can apply to all sessions, occasions, events, and circumstances.

You've no doubt heard of "the code." It's usually referenced in manly, strong, silent-type dictums: You don't screw your pal. You don't screw your pal's girlfriend. Never complain, never explain. No pain, no gain.

You could, I suppose, snatch one of those little homespun homilies as your own. Or you could adhere to a bona fide philosophy espoused by an accredited, time-tested, aesthetic, cosmological, or metaphysical philosopher such as Socrates ("An unexamined life is not worth living"); Confucius ("Since you yourself desire standing, then help others achieve it; since you yourself desire success, then help others attain it"); Rene Descartes ("I think; therefore, I am"); or Immanuel Kant ("Perception is reality"). You might even prefer to embrace an entire philosophical school, such as Stoicism, Skepticism, or Existentialism ("Life is without inherent meaning; the individual defines everything"), or fall in with one of the latter's discrete district branches (those propounded by Hegel, Kierkegaard, Sartre, and Kafka). Some of you might cast your lot with more theologically based (Judeo-Christian, Islamic, or Buddhist) philosophies.

Still others might choose to park their tenet somewhere between catchy sloganeer and high-brow dialectician. That would be in the vicinity of erudite epigrammatists like Mark Twain ("Always do right; this will gratify some people and astonish the rest"), Ralph Waldo Emerson ("Grow angry slowly—there's plenty of time"), G. K. Chesterton ("Never invoke the gods unless you really want them to appear. It annoys them very much"), or Mick Jagger ("It's all right letting yourself go, as long as you can get yourself back").

♦　　♦　　♦

Me? I'm most comforted these days with this combination platitude:

"Don't pray when it rains if you don't pray when the sun shines." (Satchel Paige)

"Keep pushing the rock up the hill." (Sisyphus)

"Add some music to your day." (Brian Wilson)

76. Be fearless (or at least pretend to be)

A gambler's ace is his ability to think clearly under stress. That's very important, because, you see, fear is the basis of all mankind. In cards, you psych 'em out, you shark 'em, you put the fear of God in 'em. That's life. —"Pug" Pierson

Perhaps the toughest bluff to pull off is that first time when you enter a roomful of strangers on opening night. Your ticker is thwacking out a 20-beat-per-second drum solo. Your pores are pouring perspiration. Your nervousness could not be any more palpable—to you.

♥ ♥ ♥

During these same moments, everyone else (unless they're unfeeling sociopaths) is going through their own jitters, preoccupied with trying to conceal their inmost anxieties from the other players. And so, when the curtain rises, there you all are: an apparently composed, prepared group of actors eager to make their mark. If any of you are feeling anything less than 100 percent, it's evident only to the most trained eye. At that point, it doesn't matter what the reviews say; you've already succeeded in the part. You've already accomplished one of the most difficult obstacles facing any neophyte: You've faced fear, and yet you're still willing to go on.

That is all you can ever ask of yourself.

Pokerese

misdeal (*n* or *v*): declared when there is some infraction caused by the dealer; the dealer then re-deals the hand.

muck (*n* or *v*): the discard pile; or when a player tosses his excess (or folded) cards. Any cards that are in the muck, or are mucked, are ineligible to win a pot.

77. Overrating the competition beats underrating it

The commonest mistake in history is underestimating your opponent; happens in poker all the time. —David Shoup, General (USMC), World War II Medal of Honor recipient (and an excellent poker player)

H
ere's an example of this principle in action:

It was Day Six of the U.S. Poker Championship at the Trump Taj Majal in Atlantic City, about an hour into the one-day 7-Card Stud High-Low event; and, at table 52, seat 2, some sap is staring into the laser glare behind the rose-colored shades of Thuan ("Scotty") Nguyen, the winner of the final 1998 WSOP Texas Hold-'Em Championship event and one of the top players on the planet. Until said sap's bump, Scotty had been bored and distracted, reading through a magazine and glancing at several of the overhead TV monitors that lined the walls of the 18,000-square-foot poker room. Admittedly the $32,000 first-place prize was a pittance compared to the $1 million (and the priceless champion bracelet) he'd won for beating the world's best. But why waste any of your valuable time or money if you're not going to take the investment seriously?

Certainly the sap was serious. He (okay, I) had never tested his (my) skills in tournament play. The plan was to lie low and tight in the early going and loosen up as the day, and the stakes, progressed; a $500 bankroll could easily be wiped out with one bad beat. By raising into the world champ, however, I was no longer lurking in the shadows. I'd proclaimed my presence. Attention, and my bet, must be paid. Nguyen called. When everyone else folded, it was just the two of us, mano a mano, chips to chips.

We both had two cards on board: Scotty showed the four of hearts and a diamond deuce; I had a three and a five, both spades. Nguyen bet the forced minimum of $5, and I immediately upped him to $15. He smiled tightly and reached for his stack. I'd seen the thin grin and that slick move before—on TV, in the constant replay of his deadly, methodical (one might even call it "arrogant") endgame over a clearly overmatched opponent. Like a pitcher tossing to first to see if the batter squares to bunt, Scotty was trying to determine if I would prematurely tip my hand by going for my chips to raise, or by staying at arm's length, possibly to fold. I watched him shake-and-fake, and I didn't flinch. So he called. Next up: six of clubs for him, ace of spades for me to go with the three and five—a possible straight flush. It was his turn to bet, and I raised. He quickly bumped back with $30, strictly an intimidation move. I had better cards on board, so he was just seeing if I showed any weakness. I said: "Raise $30." All bets were off right there; he was toast. With my possible straight flush wheel showing, he couldn't take a chance I'd fill in. Also, there was no percentage in playing with just two players' money. He threw in his cards. To give him something to think about, I flashed my two down cards: an 8 and another 3. I had bluffed out a world champ with a hand consisting of, in the poker parlance, bupkis. (It would've made a much better story if we later squared off in an even more dramatic showdown for all the marbles. But, alas, it wasn't his day. Or mine. At 12:10, after only 70 minutes of play, Scotty was one of the first players to tap out. I cruised for a while longer, winning some, losing a couple, trying to build the cushion I'd need to withstand the higher betting limits. But I soon got sucked in on a mediocre hand, eventually losing to a rank amateur who pulled the case ace on the river for a heart flush and a 7-low. It was around 2 P.M. when I became the 42nd player to fall.)

The point is this:

Poker pros (or self-proclaimed "experts") are an arrogant bunch; their shit don't stink, and yours barely rates a sniff on the chip heap. That can be a big edge for an unknown quantity like, say, you. If they expect nothing from you, it won't take much to surprise them. And surprise has been the enemy of overconfident competitors from Day One (e.g., Goliath; the hare; 1948 Dewey supporters; 1980 Russian hockey team; 2003 WSOP players, and pundits who maintained to the last stack that Chris Moneymaker was in over his head).

♠   ♠   ♠

There's little to lose if you err on the benefit-of-the-doubt, give-a-sucker-an-even-break side. Isn't it worth a tad of your time and energy to conclude that a particular opponent is no real rival? When the stakes are high, it never pays to be on the short end of a gross under-evaluation.

Remember Felix's chalkboard lesson to Oscar on *The Odd Couple*? "Assume nothing. When you assume, you can make an 'ass' of 'u' and 'me.'" Suspect (and respect) everyone and everything until you've completed your due diligence.

Two words: "Drive Defensively." By far, those two words make up the best road rule ever devised. Pure genius. In poker, you don't want to think or act defensively; however, you can't go on the full offensive until you're sure that some amateur won't come of out nowhere and sideswipe you on the turn. In other words: Look both ways before making your move.

Pokerese

No Limit (*adj* or *n*): a game in which you can bet or raise any amount at any time. In most games (and almost all tournaments), players can only bet as much as they have in front of them; if someone bets more than they have, they can still choose to call (going **all in**) and await the outcome. If they lose, they're out; if they win, they stay.

78. Kill 'em with kindness

It's a helluva thing, killing a man. You take away everything he's got in life, and everything he'll ever have.
—Clint Eastwood, actor, as William Munny in *Unforgiven*

The poker and "real" worlds are similar in many ways. They can be cold, unforgiving landscapes inhospitable to newcomers (unless they're suckers with big bucks).

The haughtiness of the anointed is a given. Less understandable is the unearned smugness of those narrow-minded, crackbrained yobs who stink at pretty much everything they do. The best you can say about them is they're here. ("We're onboard; you can pull up the gangplank.") They seem to have conveniently forgotten that there was a time when they were someplace else, isolated and alone. Shouldn't they remember that desolate, crappy feeling and try to prevent others from going through it? Show a little compassion, little people.

♥   ♥   ♥

No, I'm not going soft. I'm not suggesting that there should be a welcoming committee at every poker table. It's still big-dog-eat-little-dog when the bell sounds. But there's no reason why the casino or home environment could not encourage more civility and humility. You can still be a killer, just a kindly, more companionable one.

Pokerese

nuts (*n*): the best possible hand a player can have, mostly used in board games such as Texas Hold 'Em and Omaha. (See also **lock**.)

79. In poker, but not in life (and vice versa)

The only time we aren't in the action is when we're sleeping.
—Johnny Chan

As similar as they may be, poker and life are not identical. Differences do appear. In poker:

You can screw your friends.

You can screw your friends' partners.

You have no friends.

You have no partners.

Whereas, in life:

You need friends (who else is going to help you move?)

You don't screw them (or their friends and partners) for the same reason (above).

♣   ♣   ♣

Here are some other fundamental ways in which poker and life diverge.

In Poker	In Life
The only thing that matters is winning (money).	Four out of five major religions agree: Coming in second or third every now and again is preferable to spending eternal damnation in Hell. (And 99 out of 100 hedonists will tell you: sex and love are as good, if not better, than cash.)
Emotions are a liability. Happy, sad, empathic or angry—none of them are going to change the cards you're dealt. What they will do, however, is cloud your judgment, make you chase with garbage and leave you with empty pockets sticking up like rabbit ears.	You're never more alive than when you're feeling something… anything. Without happiness, sadness, empathy, anger, passion, jealousy, affection, anxiety, disdain, tenderness, regret, perceptivity, excitability, receptivity irritation or titillation, you're little more than . . . a Vulcan.
There is no such thing as luck. This might be especially hard to believe if you watch TV tournaments, where every Hold 'Em hand comes down to a showdown in which the hot player (usually a mouthy young jerk) fills in with the case card (a 4% possibiity) on the river. Think of it as good editing.	The fates are equally disinterested and uninterested here, too. Who can explain governing forces that continue to green-light Jackie Chan movies and yet ban Roman Polanski from entering this country. And if rubbing a four-leaf clover every day for two years has no power, how come the weekend affair with your girlfriend's Finnish cousin has never come to light. Who do you thank if not a lucky star?

In Poker	In Life
Heed the experts. There's a reason why Doyle Brunson, well into his 70s, is still showing up at final tables and beating some of those irritating kids. (and why his *Super System* is still selling 25 years after it was first published. Some genuine articles do last.	There are no experts, just shills pushing their latest book, TV show, 12- step program or exclusive line of branded coffee mugs.

80. Time is money

Begin at the beginning and go on until you come to the end; then stop.—Lewis Carroll, author, *Alice in Wonderland*

What's your limit? Tournament toughs can play for 8, 10, 15 hours straight without losing any of their concentration. Others need frequent breaks to stay sharp. Some players won't stray too far from home, knowing that they can't sustain their acuity over a long duration (or that they need too frequent breaks).

Wherever, or whatever, the game, you need to estimate how long you can keep (it) up without losing any of your optimum physical or mental stamina. Then stick close to your parameters. You can squander all you've earned by sticking around past your prime.

♥ ♥ ♥

You can and should push it, training in the same systematic way—via intervals—that elite athletes do to expand their boundaries. Find the outer edge of your comfort zone, and then try to extend it. Each session, add five minutes. (To facilitate your workout regiment, sleep, eat, and defecate more productively. And don't forget to lay off that turkey on game day.) Gauge your progress. Soon you'll have it—your exact right time. And once it's determined, don't let anything—peer coercion or foolish bravado—push you past your limits.

Pokerese

Omaha (*n*): a variation (similar to Texas Hold 'Em) in which each player is dealt four hole cards (instead of two) to go with the five community cards (dealt and bet the same as in Hold 'Em). However, to make a five-card hand, you must use only *two* hole cards and *three* board cards. (In most Hi-Lo versions, an eight or better must qualify for the best low hand.)

outs (*n*): the number of cards that will improve your hand to make it a winner. (If you have an open-ended straight, eight cards in the deck will help you fill it; therefore, you have eight outs.)

81. Make the necessary adjustments

Nobody can foresee what will please the critics. Every artistic activity is, and always will be, a poker game. —Marlene Dietrich, actress, *A Foreign Affair*

No one is immune to loss. You will suffer your allotment. You'll get hammered, nailed, and sawed into pulp. You'll get eaten and spit out. You'll get browbeaten into plowshares. (Huh? Okay, one metaphor too far.) The point is: There may even be those days when you'll come to believe that the entire universe has conspired to take away everything (and everyone) you hold near and dear.

What do you do?

After you get burnt a few times in a row, take a break. Get up, wash your face, maybe sit out a hand.

You may even seek solace in the notion that there'll be another, a better, day. But there are still another few hours to weather.

Continue to play your game. You definitely do not take greater risks because you're down. If anything, you may play a bit tighter until you can get a few wins under your belt.

What if you continue to give your all and it's still not enough?

Give some more.

The easiest thing to do when everything else fails is to acquiesce to feelings of self-pity, self-loathing, or self-flagellation.

You know the feeling. (Let's be honest: The sensation is not entirely unpleasant. No more pain. No more hurt. No more blood, sweat, tears, or toil. After you keep hitting your head against a wall, it's a welcome relief when you stop. They don't call it "sweet" surrender for nothing.)

If what you usually do is not working, fix it. Mix it up. Try something new or different. Try anything.

Adjusting to change is rarely easy. The mere thought of remodeling, reshaping, regeneration, or revolution can turn heroes to cowards. But only through being tested, and passing those tests, can true growth occur.

You may have to talk yourself through it. Remind yourself:

The cards have no memory.

The better players will ultimately defeat the lesser players.

There is no such thing as luck, but it (fate, fortune, karma, whatever) will soon turn in your favor.

♦   ♦   ♦

82. Some days it's just not your night

What do I like the most about the game of poker? Beating boys.
—Nicole Sullivan, actress, *Mad TV*

Boy, what do you do when you've done everything you can possibly do, and you still can't buy a winning hand? What do you do when justice takes a holiday? Start preparing an exit strategy.

Remember Principle No. 80? You've allocated and reached your time limit; you get up to leave, and the rest of the table entreats you to "stay just a little longer." When that doesn't work, they attack your manhood, your parentage, your loyalty to the game. But you ignore their entreaties because they're thieving, scheming, two-faced opportunists.

You're decided to leave because it's in your best interest, not theirs. And as long as you've given fair notice (at least once around the table), you're free to go.

So what's stopping you?

Pokerese

pat (*adj*): in draw, when a player keeps all five initially dealt cards, as if no other card can improve the hand (you have to pay to find out).

pig (*n*): when a player declares "both" in high-low. (In most games, you must win both ways—no ties even—to take the entire pot.) (See **scoop**.)

pocket rockets (*n*): slang for a pair of aces in the hole (most often used in Hold 'Em).

83. Winners do quit, and quitters do win

Winning isn't everything, it's the only thing.
—attributed to Vince Lombardi

Jersey-born-and-buried Vince Lombardi, who coached the Green Bay Packers to five NFL titles and won the first two Super Bowls (1967-68), died in 1970 as pro football's figurative five-star field general with a winning percentage of .740 (105-35-6). The Super Bowl trophy was named in his honor. But his biggest influence on the coaching fraternity may be as the poster boy for memorable sayings.

Many of the following quotations can still be found tacked up on the walls of high school gyms:

Success demands singleness of purpose.

To achieve success, whatever the job we have, we must pay a price.

Once a man has made a commitment to a way of life, nothing will stop him short of success.

The harder you work, the harder it is to surrender.

Battles are primarily won in the hearts of men.

You've got to win the war with the man in front of you. You've got to get your man.

The good Lord gave you a body that can stand most anything. It's your mind you have to convince.

Mental toughness is essential to success.

Mental toughness is a state of mind. You could call it character in action.

It's easy to have faith in yourself and have discipline when you're number one. What you've got to have is faith and discipline when you're not yet a winner.

I firmly believe that any man's finest hour, the greatest fulfillment of all that he holds dear, is the moment when he has worked his heart out in a good cause and lies exhausted on the field of battle, victorious.

In great attempts, it is glorious even to fail.

If it doesn't matter who wins or loses, then why do they keep score?

Once you learn to quit, it becomes a habit.

Winning isn't everything, it's the only thing.

The thing is: Much like Yogi Berra was given credit for dozens more amazingly amusing, quasi-brilliant sayings than he actually said, Lombardi's quotes were often pepped up, if not actually piped, by adoring acolytes. Such as arguably his most famous paradigm: "Winning isn't everything, it's the only thing." His actual words were: "Winning isn't everything, but wanting to is."

Another problem is that some of the things Lombardi said were simplistic, semi-militaristic jargon, which does not play as well as it once did. Such as: "Winners never quit and quitters never win."

There is a time and a place to quit. It comes after you've given your all and it's still not enough. It comes after you've tapped some reserve of hidden strength and courage when it seems like you had nothing left in your tank. It comes after you've made your adjustments and you've exhausted your mental and physical resources.

Winners do quit. You must. To keep on absorbing punishment would be foolish and masochistic—two qualities never to be found in successful poker players.

You fight till the last, but no longer.

You stop hitting your head against the wall, and you hit the bricks to fight another day.

Pokerese

position (*n*): respective location of each player at the table when it comes to act (which changes on each hand). As a rule, early positions are at a disadvantage since they must make their play first. (Also, individuals tend to play tighter in an early position, looser in a late position.)

84. It's not (exactly) gambling

God does not play dice with the universe: He plays an ineffable game of His own devising, which might be compared, from the perspective of any of the other players [i.e. everybody], to being involved in an obscure and complex variant of poker in a pitch-dark room, with blank cards, for infinite stakes, with a Dealer who won't tell you the rules, and who smiles all the time.
—Terry Pratchett and Neil Gaiman, authors, *Good Omens*

"Have a good time gambling . . ."

It's one thing to hear that when you go off to a casino to play craps, blackjack, baccarat or, especially, roulette. It's quite another to hear that before you head out to your regular card game.

No doubt you've tried on innumerable occasions to explain the differences between games of chance and games of skill, but I'll wager you haven't had much luck getting through.

Allow me.

Gambling is, by definition, any enterprise in which you bet (money or property) on an uncertain outcome. Since few outcomes are absolutely, bet-the-farm, 150-percent certain, then strictly speaking, every time you back up your hunches, suppositions, beliefs, and actions with some sort of stakes, you're gambling. But let's penetrate and parse a little deeper. Take, say, horse racing (the flats, not the obviously tampered, if not actually fixed, trotters).

As approached by the typical punter, the sport of kings remains an unlockable mystery that rarely allows itself to be accurately and prosperously handicapped. Some touts are better than others at assessing hard data, but few are well equipped to gauge intangibles such as mud, heart, and the human element. In this field, unless you have firsthand, probably illicit information, there is no such thing as a sure thing.

However . . .

There is something called form ("according to form" . . . "true to form" . . . "if form holds" . . .) that relies on empirical evidence and probability to predict results with near certitude. It is form that determines the odds. It is form that long shots strive to overcome. It is form that is proven correct when, nine times out of ten, the top-seeded tennis tour professional defeats the unseeded club pro. But it is the tenth time that lends the outcome that tiny, improbable smidge of uncertainty.

♣   ♣   ♣

So, in poker?

On the random day or night, any fish (moron) can win, but it is 151-percent certain that, over the long run of weeks, months, and—definitely—years, the skillful player (with his greater blend of wits, wiles, guts, and guile) will leave the table much more cash-enriched.

All other things being equal, that outcome is certain. Therefore, poker is not gambling per se. There is no house edge. The difference in play is strictly confined to that human element, and the choices you make regarding the cards you're dealt. What could be fairer? Just you and your disciplined instincts making calculated risks for fun and profit.

"You're playing cards tonight, Honey? Have a good time skillfully beating inferior competition."

Pokerese

pot limit (*n*): game stakes, in which a player's maximum bet or raise is equal to the size of the current pot.

85. It's for the money (and the girls)

It's not for the girls, and it's not for the money. It's for the glory.
—Larry Olmstead, record holder—72 hours—of the longest single casino poker session

We appreciate your feat and all, Larry. It's not every day that, just four months after traveling the farthest distance—7,500 miles, from Australia to California—to play back-to-back golf rounds, a 38-year-old man from Vermont could sit for three days straight (with only 15-minute breaks every eight hours to change clothes and brush his teeth) at the seven-card stud table in the Foxwoods Resort Casino (Mashantucket, Connecticut). The most impressive aspect of your record-setting sit, Larry, was that you did more than just take up space for 72 hours; you won nearly $1,000 for your time. But the comment you made (above)—after generously donating most of your winnings to the Foxwoods' staff—must be rebuked. Considering your fragile state at the time, we'll go easy:

♦   ♦   ♦

Larry, you're wrong. It's never about the glory. Trophies and certificates are worth nothing beyond appearances. And appearances, like pride and glory, have no intrinsic value; they are false gods.

It's always about the money. It's how you keep score. You can take it to the bank. And you can use it to feed the bulldog.

As for the women—or the men, depending on one's preference—it's almost as often about them. Because what you do for money, if you're lucky, you also do for love.

Pokerese

prop player (*n*): employed by the house to fill in when a game runs short of players.

86. All's fair

All is fair in love, war, and poker. —William J. Florence

I t is a fierce, strategic, often epic, struggle out there—not for hearts or minds but for money and property. And yet, what a great and beautiful war it is when no combatants are killed.

Still, you need a killer instinct to prevail. It's like Amarillo Slim says: "I'll put a rattlesnake in your pocket, and ask you for a match."

Do you have whatever it takes, within the spirit and letter of the law, to put a rattlesnake in your friend's pocket or kick your neighbor's ass from here to eternity?

♣ ♣ ♣

If you hesitated for a moment in response, you probably don't have what it takes.

There's no shame in being born without a sneaky, vicious bone in your body. And, as for being made into a sharklike entity, if you were not imbued with this disposition from birth, conserve your energy.

Save the whales instead. You can't create a stone-cold monster from a warmly compassionate mensch.

Many healthy, successful people, however, are capable of grasping complex, even diametrically opposed, thoughts simultaneously. They're among the fortunate men and women who can seamlessly shift from cat to mouse with nary a peep. They can be both mensch and killer. They can compete and play with controlled, monstrous aggression, and they can also nurture and love with complete and utter selflessness.

Pokerese

qualifier (*n*): a minimum standard that a hand must meet in order to play or win (such as in Jacks or Better, or Eights or Better).

87. It is a sport

Poker has been around a long time. It should be a sport.
—Raymond Bitar, CEO of TiltWare, a gaming software company

Some self-interested suit (above) claims that longevity should be a key criterion for an activity's inclusion in the Olympics. Well, I guess that nails that. Stargazing? Olympic sport. Cave painting, firebuilding, and wheelmaking? Sport, sport, and sport. Fornicating? Urinating? (Hmm. Think of the competitive possibilities.)

♥   ♥   ♥

In all fairness, there are some legitimate arguments to consider. And, in all laziness, let's start with the dictionary definition: **Sport** (n): (*1.*) *an active pastime; diversion; recreation.* All words (with the possible exception of "active") point go. (*2.*) *a specific diversion, usually involving physical exercise and having a set form and body of rules; a game.* Another mixed, but positively weighted, bag:

☑ specific diversion;

☑ set form;

☑ body of rules;

☑ a game;

☒ usually involving physical exercise.

Again, nothing definitive one way or the other, so let's break it down by examining some of the components commonly present in all accepted sports:

Betting. Not only do fans wager on the outcome, players do, too (it's not only allowed, it's part of the game).

Pressure. There's arguably more tension and stress in poker than in most sports' professional ranks. In poker, you don't get paid if you don't win (in most tournaments, you have to shell out money just to play). In basketball, Kobe Bryant will make $136 million over seven years (that's nearly $240,000 per regular-season game) whether he suits up or not.

Prize money. If you do win, however, you can make a small fortune. Greg Raymer, 2004 World Series of Poker champion, took home $5 million. (A total of $20 million was awarded in official prize money, and probably twice that figure was wagered in "unofficial" competition.)

Media saturation. Its tournaments are a staple of several TV networks, including Bravo, the Travel Channel and—this is the pro-sport kicker—ESPN.

Mental toughness. Discipline, concentration, and overcoming adversity are the requisites for every first-rate player.

Physical challenge. Winning the World Series of Poker requires six consecutive days of 12- to 15-hour daily, heart-thumping, adrenaline-pumping, perspiration-inducing play (with a 10-minute bathroom break every two hours). Winning the Major League Baseball World Series requires four to seven days of nonconsecutive play (rarely more than three hours in any one day) with bathroom breaks available every half-inning.

Comparisons. Purists differ on whether or not badminton, curling, archery, and synchronized swimming should be considered sports, yet all are part of the Olympic Games. Others refuse to accept the legitimacy of bowling, darts, golf, and automobile racing. (Counterclaim: If a participant can die in his/her pastime—as in racing and, on rare occasions, darts—it's a sport.)

Two final words: rhythmic gymnastics.

Pokerese

railbird (*n*): a person (a fan, relative or a tapped-out player) standing near an active table (usually in a tournament) to watch, root, or kibitz.

88. It is not a sport

Poker is not a sport. —Tony Kornheiser, newspaper columnist/
radio personality/TV host, *Pardon the Interruption*

M r. Kornheiser is a terrific writer and a provocative media personality. He also speaks for most middle-aged, bald, overweight, sports-minded men (many of whom, no doubt, play poker). However, if his sole say-so is not sufficient, look to architects of the Ancient and Modern Games, the Greeks. They had the most advanced schools of philosophy and advanced mathematics of their era, yet they did not see fit to include any "intellectual" games in their Olympics.

♠   ♠   ♠

And just because it's televised on ESPN (Every Sane Person's Nightmare) doesn't make it a sport. Spelling Bees? Scrabble?

89. Friendly games do exist

In order to maintain your charm of manner in a poker game I suggest that you win. But if you lose, be a cheerful loser. After all, what have you lost? Just money. —Russell Crouse

Amicable contests are out there. They're there for those individuals who don't care about money or competition or pride or honor. They're there for those individuals who can completely compartmentalize their thoughts and actions (and those of their competitors). They're there for those individuals who take absolutely nothing personally. They're there for those individuals who are more interested in perfectly theoretical, as opposed to actual, play. They're there for those individuals who can be bluffed out with matchsticks.

♣　　♣　　♣

There's a name for these games and their friendly practitioners: fictitious.

90. There is no such thing as a friendly game (if you want to remain friends)

Don't jump on a man unless he's down. —Finley Peter Dunne

In the material world, all wars have casualties.

♦ ♦ ♦

You might want to make a mental note the next time you're about to sit down and play for live ammunition with your minister, priest, rabbi, guru, employer, employee, colleague, wife, husband, mate, relative, friend, or with anyone you might one day need for a reference.

91. Check and raise

Poker is a fighting game, a game in which each player tries to get the better of every other player and does so by fair means or foul so long as he obeys the rules of the game. ... It probably began as a war game; that is, the representation of a miniature battle between the forces of two kingdoms.

—Karl Menninger, psychologist/author, *Love Against Hate*

Let's review: Your approach should be businesslike, stoic, nonconfrontational, philosophical, variegated, disciplined, perceptive, self-aware, ruthless, upright, honest, well-schooled, well-financed, well-conditioned, respectful, cheerful, poetic, groovy, ballsy, anticipatory, profane, controlling, manipulative, fearless, kind, competitive, sporting, accepting, and observational. Plus, never play cards with a man named Doc, never eat at a place called Mom's, never sleep with a woman whose troubles are worse than your own. And never say never. Once you've internalized these salient nuggets, you're ready for the true demarcation between relatively amiable and seriously cutthroat play (in addition to the higher stakes): check and raise.

It is hostile, piratical deception to pretend to play nice under a friendly (or even a white) flag and then BAM!—when you've got your enemy to lower his guard—show your true colors and fire at will. Check-raise may be the most emblematic move in poker. It's only a picnic when you've got a knife, a fork, and a big appetite.

♠   ♠   ♠

You kids raised on TV might not know it, but there used to be an unwritten rule in most gentlemen's games that you did not hustle your opponents. In poker that came to mean one main thing: no check-raising. Silly rule. We now know that check-raising is an integral part, an essential piece, and a key component to the spirit and letter of the game.

Pokerese

rake (*n*): the amount of each pot the house takes for hosting a game.

92. It's lonely at the top

Don't believe the world owes you a living; the world owes you nothing—it was here first. —Robert Burdette, author, *The Drums of the 47th*

You're not whining, are you?

You worked damned long and hard to get here.

You gave twice as good as you got.

You became a target, took their best shots, and you're still standing.

So, what's the problem?

Yes, it's tiring and tiresome to withstand the tilt-aimed barbs slung your way by men and women who would be king. And sure, it's only human to desire some kind word or gesture now and then. Who wouldn't want to be acknowledged for dynastic achievement? But if there's no tea and sympathy when your mother croaks, don't imagine you'll find much pity for your empty, companionless, isolated perch in the rarefied, reclusive air above the rabble.

♣   ♣   ♣

When you accept the mantle of champ (even if it's only to lord over a $2 to $4 poker game), you must prepare yourself for these (Look Out For) Number One lessons:

If you're above, then everyone else is below.

Everyone else is gunning for you.

Only your loved ones have your back (and I'd still look behind you now and then).

During competition, there is no love lost or found. (Before and after, yes. During, never.)

Your fortunes can change in the blink of an eye, the tick of a stock point, or the turn of a card.

When your desire wanes, so does your position.

No one stays Number One by thinking too much about numbers two, three, and four.

Pokerese

river (*n*): the fifth and final community card in board games like Hold 'Em or Omaha. Also known as fifth street.

93. Don't believe the hype

We have to quit reading about everyone that thinks we're so good. You don't win on paper, you win on the football field. —Jim Beeson, high school football coach, before beating an opponent, 75-21

Form and probability do count for something, but the gazillions of other cliché mongers who've had similar things to say about hype (Don't believe it) and paper (Games are not played on it) are right. Only reputations are won and lost in the media. Games are decided on tangible surfaces such as grass, concrete, sand, wood, Har-Tru, Astroturf, linoleum, and felt (among others).

♦　　♦　　♦

If you believe everything you hear or read before a matchup, you're a gullible sap who still bets Goliath as a lock. Not everyone called Killer is doing hard time, and Tiny is usually closer to a 300-pound behemoth than a microscopic organism. The poker world is especially lax in policing its nicknames; too often, you'll find that a player has dubbed himself (a no-no of such gargantuan scale that "Low-Life Two-Faced Weasel" or "Classless Four-Flushing Puissant" can't begin to counter). Accept your enemy's intel on the upcoming battle, and you'll find yourself on the short end at Waterloo, Little Big Horn, or Fenway Park.

If you think of an opponent as "unbeatable," what chance do you have of beating him? (Two chances: slim and none.) (You don't want to buy into his "patsy" label either; you'll end up on your overconfident ass.)

Believe only in yourself and what you know to be true.

Always, always, always play your game (there's a good reason why it's your game).

Pokerese

scoop (*n* or *v*): when a playing declares "both" or "pig" in a high-low game, and wins, he *scoops* the entire pot.

94. Defeat is a better teacher than victory

Every defeat, every heartbreak, every loss, contains its own seed, its own lesson on how to improve your performance the next time. —Og Mandino, self-improvement autho, (25 million books, in 18 languages, sold)

You don't dwell on defeat, but you do well to study it. Consider every angle from every perspective. School yourself on how or why you failed and what you can do to prevent the same conclusion from recurring.

If not?

"Those who do not learn from history are doomed to repeat it."
—George Santayana, philosopher

♠ ♠ ♠

Think only of Wily Coyote.

Cartoon after cartoon, afternoon after afternoon, doom after doom. First runs and repeats make no difference. *Wily* Coyote? The poor dense critter inevitably meets the same disheartening fate. What a waste for a cat who has such energy, such imagination, such . . . a learning disability. How else to explain his oh-so-close defeat time and again, time and again? You think the Roadrunner is such a genius? He's a big beeping turd. He's fast, you gotta give him that. But he would've been stomped, crushed, or eaten long ago if the doomed-fool Coyote had learned and applied just one damned thing from his mistakes.

Pokerese

tight (*adj*): characterizes players who are cautious (some might say overly so), and usually stay in a hand only when they have excellent cards.

tilt (*n* or *v*): to play wildly or recklessly, often after a bad beat; or when another player's needling hits its mark. An out-of-control player is said to be "on tilt."

95. Don't play to the crowd

Please all, and you will please none. —Aesop, author, *Fables*

Take a look at what passes for popular in contemporary entertainment, literature, politics, and sports. Any objective observer must conclude that the masses are tasteless, mindless, second-rate-loving boobs and/or fickle, lowest-common-denominating, fair-weather fans. We seem now to be passing through a phase in which the public seems most intent on watching its own—the more ordinary the better—outthink, outdo, outfight, outrage, outgross, outlast, and outeat its own. As soon as an idea sticks in our consciousness, three similar ones appear, vying for the same audience.

Look no further than the gentrification of poker. The game has become an industry juggernaut, sweeping through the public consciousness with new- and old-media marketing savvy, everyone seemingly getting his/her fair share of the pie. Want milk? Uh, there are signs already that the cash cow might be squeezed dry.

Televising tournament poker was a good idea whose viability became great with the invention of the "pocket cam." One, two, three, then four cable TV networks made their play with slight variations until poker programming became a linchpin of each net's lineup.

That's a lot of product but only a finite amount of recognizable figures. "Characters" had to be created. Celebrities were tossed in and out of the mix. Aspiring reality-TV "stars" got the message that there were two ways for them to cash in: prize money and face time. Breakout personalities invariably resulted more from some hook—a recognizable gimmick, prop, or signature tagline—than a particular skill. Ability was trumped by marketability.

Poker's best (and worst) have also seen the light, and begun to pander to the same public that considers eating a bowl of white hairy worms a feat. More and more, they're playing to the crowd, their audience, as much (or more) as the opposition. They don't yet realize that, by pandering so baldly for P.D.A., they're halving their shelf life. The more they're out there, the sooner the public will shift their affections elsewhere.

♥   ♥   ♥

Do you really think the railbirds care if you win or lose? Why should they? What do they get out of the deal? Are you giving them a cut of the action?

So? (Here comes the self-help advice.)

Please stop trying to please the audience. Be yourself, even if you're a sullen, snide, sore loser.

Please lose the goofy glasses, the stupid hats, and the even stupider sweatshirt hoods. Lose all of the freakin' trademarks (they're *so* played out). Lose the attitude, the self-made nicknames, the trash-brash-talking schtick.

Please shut up and deal.

And? (Here's the moralizing to this story.)

Winners are not (nor should they be) always cheered. You're not a bona fide big leaguer until you've been booed. Take the less-traveled road. Go your own way. Screw 'em if they can't take a joke.

Pokerese

turn (*n*): the fourth community card in a board game such as Hold 'Em or Omaha. Also known as **fourth street**.

---

wheel (*n*): a hand that includes A, 2, 3, 4, 5 (a straight to the five) and, in games that allow straights and flushes to go both high and low, the best low.

96. If you chase two pigeons, both will escape

What's the difference between a good player and a great player?
Concentration and management of his money.
—Jimmy "the Greek" Snyder, oddsmaker and gambler

Keep your eyes on the prize. If you lose sight of your primary goal, you'll lose track of your priorities. Lose track, you'll lose concentration and focus. Lose concentration and focus, you'll lose time. Lose time, and you'll likely lose money.

The point has been made earlier, but it is worth repeating as a rule within a rule:

PLAY THE GAME, NOT YOUR MAN.

Or as a rule within rule within a rule:

STICK TO YOUR GAME PLAN; DON'T STICK IT TO A (OR THE) MAN.

After 95 discrete principles, I might be losing a little

concentration. (So, I'm gonna take a break: hit the head, then the sack for a few winks.)

♣   ♣   ♣

Now I'm back—focused, alert, stronger than ever.

You can't let your attentions wander for too long without a wakeup call. And that is the aim: single-minded purpose. If you're there to win money, do it; stop trying to win friends (or enemies). Don't waste a tick's breath thinking about that front-running wiseass who screams and points to his posse after every winning hand, or the sandbagging weasel who seems to have made you his primary target, or the over-rated two-time champion who's lucked out on pigeon plays too many times to count.

You could go round (and round) the table chasing your tail, but you won't. Revenge actions will strengthen not only your purported target but every other wiseass, weasel, and pigeon at the table. By not isolating any particular species, you'll be able to keep an eye on all of the them. Extraneous moves will break your rhythm and play into the hands of your wiliest, most nefarious competitors. Showy play will only lead you far, far away from your game plan, which is the last place you want to be.

Snap instead to total attention and do whatever it takes to be the last person standing (if it's a life metaphor; *sitting*, if it's in a poker context).

97. Enjoy the process

I stayed up all night playing poker with tarot cards. I got a full house and four people died. —Steven Wright, writer/actor/comedian

Y ou can't be truly successful if you don't derive pleasure from what you're doing. Love what (or who) you're doing, or don't do it (him/her). Move on. Find something or someone else.

♦ ♦ ♦

In this regard, life and poker are interchangeable. They're both much too long when times are tough, and much too short when the going's good.

98. Plan for the worst, hope for the best

The probability of being dealt a pair of Aces before the flop in Texas Hold 'Em is 0.45 percent; the odds against it are 220 to 1.
—Mike Caro

The probability of an event occurring in any single trial, on average, is expressed as a percentage. Odds tell you how many times an event will likely, all things being equal, happen and how many times it won't.

You should study the percentages and odds until you know them by heart. Then, forget about them. Because probability isn't absolute, and odds aren't definite. Because numbers can sometimes lie, and form doesn't always hold true. Because, as you well know by now: Shit happens. Justice takes a holiday. Winners lose. Losers win.

Only the nuts are a lock (and even then, you can sometimes tie). The one sure thing (in life, as well as in poker) is that there are no sure things.

By planning for the worst, you're prepared for any eventuality. You won't be surprised. You'll have a contingency plan. And by hoping for the best, your attitude will pick you up when you're down. You'll remain focused. You'll be ready to rake aplenty when the gods start smiling in your direction.

Pokerese

wired pair (*n*): any pair in the hole, dealt at the beginning of the game, most often used in seven-card stud.

zilch or zip (*n*): a hand worth nothing; nada; garbage; crapola; opposite of the **goods**.

99. You can't hit a 5-run homer on one pitch

Grow angry slowly—there's plenty of time.
—Ralph Waldo Emerson, essayist, *Self Reliance and Other Essays*

You can only do what you can. Forget those coachs' clichés about giving 150 or 200 percent; 100 percent is maximum, full-out, perfect, unattainable capacity, and anything near 98.6 is damned good output.

The cliché about one at a time—one hit/score/game/hand/step—is simply, flawlessly true. If you try to do too (two or more) much, you'll likely press and hurry. In your haste, you'll put pressure and desperation and emotion into play. You'll be holding on so dearly for life that you'll likely crash and burn.

♠   ♠   ♠

There's the oxymoronic rub: the tighter you grasp, the less power you have.

In golf (and in some automobile-driving and baseball-hitting schools), the core mantra is soft hands. Not soft as in "velvety to the touch," but soft as in "relaxed." You want to speed through the hitting zone with a perfectly easy (but-not-so-easy-that-you-lose-control), perfectly controlled (but-not-so-controlled-that-you-lose-feel) grip. In poker, the metaphor is more figurative. Calm, shift, and slow yourself down. Do only what you can do. Do only what the circumstances allow. (You're not going to win $1,000 in a $1-$3 game—that would be like a 5-run dinger—so don't even try.)

The more that's on the line, the more relaxed you should be. Smile. Whenever you feel that smile—or your grip—tightening, take a few deep inhalations and exhalations. C'mon, *really* smile. Crunch time is a blast. It's what you've been working and preparing for all this time. Steady and ready yourself for a long, patient climb. The sky's the limit as long as you take it one measured, pleasurable step at a time.

Pokerese

zombie (*n*): a player with no discernible tells, ticks, or indicator. In other words, a player you want to avoid, and definitely do not want to find across from you at a table.

100. It's over in the blink of a one-eyed jack

Here is one of the most exciting and absorbing occupations known to intelligent American manhood; here a year's reflection is compressed into a moment of thought; here the nerves may stand on end and scream to themselves —Stephen Crane, author, *A Poker Game*

I n poker, as in every engaged life, time flies. It goes beyond reflection and thought. It's as if all business and professional relationships, expressed and suppressed emotions, financial gains and losses were compressed into infinitesimally incremental sessions.

♥　　♥　　♥

If days were dollars, the hours would pass like halfpennies.

Don't scrimp, pinch, muck, or grind them out. Spend them wisely. Play each game as if it's your last.

101. Patience, and shuffle the cards

—Miguel Cervantes, author, *Don Quixote*

Amen.

♠　　♠　　♠

Index

About the Author

Lee Robert Schreiber is the author of nine previous books, including *False Glory*, a cautionary tale about steroid use in pro football (Ron Mix, NFL Hall of Famer, called it "the most important book about athletics ever written," and *Time* magazine cited Mr. Schreiber as "a brilliant rookie biographer"); and *The One That Got Away*, a memoir of his checkered dating history published earlier this year. He was included among the country's top baseball writers in *Going, Going, Gone: The History, Lore, and Mystique of the Home Run*.

The author of this entertaining, informative, how-to, self-help book supported himself through college via his instinctive wiles. He's played every variation extant (he even invented a few) at every stakes level, including no limit. In his only tournament experience, he outlasted world champion Scotty Nguyen, an account he chronicled for *Fortune Small Business*, one of numerous publications in which he's shared his poker-related wit and wisdom.